Gather Ye Wild Things

Gather Ye Wild Things

A forager's year

Susan Tyler Hitchcock

Illustrations by
G. B. McIntosh

University Press of Virginia
Charlottesville and London

THE UNIVERSITY PRESS OF VIRGINIA
Text copyright © 1980, 1995 by Susan Tyler Hitchcock
Drawings copyright © 1980, 1995 by G. B. McIntosh

First paperback edition 1995

Designed by Suzanne Haldane

Library of Congress Cataloging-in-Publication Data
Hitchcock, Susan Tyler.
    Gather ye wild things : a forager's year / Susan Tyler Hitchcock ;
illustrations by G. B. McIntosh. — 1st pbk. ed.
        p.   cm.
    Originally published: New York : Harper & Row, c1980.
    Includes bibliographical references (p. 175) and index.
    ISBN 0-8139-1643-7 (acid-free paper)
    1. Wild plants, Edible.   2. Cookery (Wild foods).   I. Title.
QK98.5.A1H57   1995
581.6′32 — dc20   95-12420
                                                           CIP

Printed in the United States of America

For Erbin: our book

Preface

IN SOME WAYS this book, written now more than fifteen years ago, feels like a relic. In other ways it feels as if it will never grow old.

I wrote then that gathering wild things can be a way of life. Then, it was for me. The study and practice of using common wild plants permeated my life in 1980, when *Gather Ye Wild Things* was first published. Back then, one friend even called me "Mother Nature." I taught weekly classes, wrote this book and many articles, published a calendar, worked with artist friends to design T-shirts (my favorite: "Go Wild — Eat Weeds"). Gathering wild things was all my life. It sounds like a contradiction, but for a few years there, I made a living of it.

Since then, so many things have changed. Within two months of the original publication of this book, I married David Watkins. In the next six years, we bought property and built a home. The land is less than ten miles from the mountainside where I roamed, day after day, learning to identify wild things. It felt familiar, and yet it belongs to us. We have spent much energy beating back the bush — yanking up blackberry bushes, cutting off sassafras suckers, sawing down the hickory tree that grew right at our front window — trying to make a haven amidst the mountain wilds.

In those years, we gave birth to two beautiful children. I hesitate to mention them in the same breath with goats, but here goes. It quickly became clear: one or the other. I remember the moment it hit me. My first child, John, was born in early summer. We often shared those middle-of-the-night nursing-mother-and-infant rendezvous.

We had one yearling goat and one Australian shepherd dog, both brown. They were fast friends. They would curl up together in the summer shade. I remember the sound, as I cradled my baby in the dark, of the goat and the dog prancing gleefully up and down the deck, playing in the midnight moonlight as energetically as if it were midday. That was it. No more goats. Given the choice between them and babies, I took my own.

I mention goats in this meditation because, as I wrote in the chapter here on clovers, they were my models, my inspiration, the epitome of the creature who relished a taste of the wild. In the days of writing *Gather Ye Wild Things*, I lived by a satisfying rhythm. The book began during the years when I was writing a doctoral dissertation, trying to unfold the spiritual vision of the poet Percy Bysshe Shelley. I would read and explicate, write and explain intensely for four or five hours in the morning. Then I would set out for the mountain slopes, accompanied by my little band of goats. They would search for greenbrier and honeysuckle; I would search for ginseng and wild ginger.

But in the 1980s, I traded in goats for infants, traded in roaming the slopes for clearing them. Gathering wild things became a familiar possibility, not the focus of my life. Sure, I would cook up a mess of poke when the stalks plumped up thick and tender. Sure, I would roam, baby in backpack, and bring back blackberries for cobbler or pie. I always let a few chickweed plants thrive, because I knew how good it would taste in spring salad, mixed with the lettuce and kale. I rejoiced the year I first found purslane sprouts in the garden.

Gathering wild things shifted, in other words, from an all-out obsession to a tempered feature of everyday life. And that's the point: you don't have to go back to nature whole hog in order to enjoy the pleasures and benefits of wild things. You don't have to live in the forest. You don't have to dig up weird roots, boil down fibrous stalks, crack open tough nuts. (Although you can, and should, if you want to — it can be quite an experience!) You can live in a suburb, grow a few flowers, and snip off a few weeds here and there.

Granted, there are limits. Once *Gather Ye Wild Things* was published I went up, book in hand, to interest the *Washington Post* food editor, Phyllis C. Richman, in a series of articles on wild things in Washington. We agreed on a set of eleven, almost a plant a month. After two articles — dandelions and violets, if I remember correctly — I got a call from Phyllis.

"Find something else to write about," she told me. "City people don't want to eat the weeds."

And I don't blame them. I'm all for weeds in the cities. It warms my heart to see mullein and mugwort in Central Park. But I don't want to gather them. Too many people sharing the space, too much junk in the air those plants are breathing. Half an hour out, though, in Westport or Alexandria, you can find plenty of tasty weeds.

I would like to believe that it has happened to others as it has happened to me: that common wild foods have simply become a part of daily life. I snip wild garlic greens to sprinkle on baked potatoes. I nibble every wild strawberry I can find. I toss the leaves of violet and lamb's quarters into the summer salad basket. When I find a clean white puffball, I fry it up on the side. I delight in each year's first soft persimmon.

And now, as my children grow older, they are learning to identify and enjoy the wild things, too. Berries didn't take much teaching. We hunted up sassafras saplings last spring, to boil down for a spring tonic tea. They learned the look of that bright green wood growing up out of the mottled brown. They learned to know the buds without the telltale leaves. Both of them chew the twigs of sweet birch and enjoy the taste of chickweed, my all-time favorite wild salad green. All these lessons have not come to them through classes or book learning, but simply through being at my side as we weed the garden or walk the woods.

That is as it should be. The wisdom of gathering wild things should be a gift passed on free from mother to child, from friend to friend, from generation to generation. Somewhere in *Gather Ye Wild Things,* I'm sure, I mourn the absence of such a wise woman in my life, someone with whom I could have been the child and the learner. I have made situations happen that almost answer that need. In 1981 my mother and I were traveling in Sussex, England, traipsing in the footsteps of Shelley. We went into a bookstore in Horsham, near his childhood home. There I saw stacks of a big, beautiful full-color book, *All Good Things around Us,* a British sort of *Gather Ye Wild Things.* I looked, and noticed that all the books were signed. I asked at the bookstore counter.

"Pamela Michael," the bookstore manager told me. "She lives nearby." We phoned her, and she instantly extended an invitation for us to come and visit. My mother and I followed her directions to a Tudor cottage, plants in abundance all around, where we met this wonderful woman and her husband, Maurice. Pamela and I talked and talked, plants and books and recipes. We were kindred spirits, we knew right away.

Two years later, Mother and I visited the Michaels again. Pamela and I took a walk on the Sussex Downs. She would stop at this plant and that, telling me names and stories. It was just one morning's walk, but what a wonderful feeling to be listening and learning from someone who loved plants as deeply as I. Our friendship grows and continues today, even though we rarely see each other and commune mostly through Christmas cards.

We continue to weave a quiet community, those of us who love wild things. It's not a movement, nothing political. It's something we feel in our hearts for each other. As the time and occasion to gather wild things has receded in my own life, I have my dear friend Kathy Jaquette to thank for keeping the thread alive. Kathy lives now in the house on the mountain-side where I lived when I wrote *Gather Ye Wild Things,* where Gail and I scrambled up steep slopes to find just the right morel mushroom, just the perfect cluster of rose hips, for her to capture in spirit and line.

Kathy loves those wild things. And herbs, and mushrooms, and fruits and nuts and greens and vegetables. She and her husband, Chris Hill, are godparents to my children and, it feels sometimes, to the child within me who still wants to run away to the wild. At their house, the line between indoors and outdoors blurs. Common weeds and tropical grasses thrive side by side in pots on the windowsill. Out on the deck, Kathy is nurturing a forest of veiny, carnivorous pitcher plants. In the yard, four-foot lengths of red oak sprout saucer-sized shiitake mushrooms.

Kathy is always reveling in the world of wild things. She and I take great pleasure, every summer, in teaming up to adorn our pretty little Cove Church with great overflowing bouquets of weeds, bringing the chaos of nature into the fold. And in late autumn, as we head toward the holidays, Kathy invites a dozen women — Gail McIntosh and myself among them — to mingle our separate harvests into potpourris, marinades, and healthful teas. We gather, brought together by the plants that we love.

I tend to assume that everyone has incorporated gathering wild things into their lives. Then I get brought up short. That happened this spring.

I was asked to make an informal presentation to a garden club in Charlottesville, the faculty wives of the University of Virginia. I offered to talk about my favorite weeds. Dandelion, violets, lamb's quarters, clovers, chickweed: that was the outline I planned to follow.

But I figured everyone knew all about these plants already. I feared it would be old hat to these women, all of them gardeners and plant lovers, living in Albemarle County, where a life in the out-of-doors is the common way.

I gave my talk, and they listened avidly. Then I took an informal poll. Of those eighteen women, only one had ever eaten a weed. A few of the women knew a few of the plants I had mentioned, but more as intruders than as welcome guests to the garden. Only one among them could identify chickweed.

One woman came up afterwards and told me she thought she ought not gather greens from her garden because of the weed killer she and her husband tended to use. I agreed with her concern. Maybe she'll think twice before killing her weeds next season.

I went away aware that I should not abandon the mission. Gathering wild things has become second nature to me, but not to everybody.

I am grateful to the University Press of Virginia and to Boyd Zenner, my editor, for bringing this book back into the light. Its immediate circumstances may have faded, but the stories it tells will last forever, as long as the green growing world of the wild prevails.

Contents

Preface   vii
Introduction   1

SPRING

Birch and Maple   9
Wild Easter Eggs   13
Redbud and Violet   15
Wild Garden Before the Plough   18
Spring Shoots   22
Sassafras   24
Cleavers   28
Sorrels   30
In Defense of Dandelions   33
Poke   36
Essence of Spring   40
Miraculous Morels   43
Wild Strawberries   46

SUMMER

Daylilies   51
Yarrow   53
Lamb's Quarters   56
Wild Herbs in the Garden   59

Cattails	62
Clovers	67
Elder Blow, Elderberries	69
Rubus Berries	72
Wild and Clean	76
Purslane	80
May Apples	83
Amaranth	85
Kudzu	88
Jewelweed vs. Poison Ivy	92
Summer Smoke	96

AUTUMN

Self-Heal	101
Wild Spice	103
Chicory	105
Autumn Teas	108
Sumac	111
Watercress	113
Puffballs	116
Wild Grapes	118
Ginseng the Inscrutable	121
Old Pomes	127
Eating Acorns	130
Wild Ginger	133
Nutting	136

WINTER

Sunflower Potatoes	143
Winter Greens	146
Rose Hips	149
Winter Sprouts	152
Persimmons	154

Wild Holidays   157
Periwinkle   159
Praying Mantis Egg Case   162
Wild Onions, Wild Garlic   164
Winter Terrarium   167
Gathering Together   171

Bibliography   175
Index   179

Introduction

GATHERING wild things can become a year-round preoccupation, a way of life. The landscape changes shape when you start noticing which plants grow where, which plants are good for what. Good-for-nothing backlots turn into fruitful havens. Weeds in the garden look as good as the vegetables. Forest underbrush begins to tell a story as intricate as an illuminated manuscript, once one takes the time to read it.

Plants can tell the story of how life was for eons, before mass-processed food and synthetic pharmaceuticals turned our attention from the land. Most Indian vocabularies included hundreds of words for plants, their parts, their growing phases, and their uses. Primitives had reason to make those discriminations: their health and livelihood depended on awareness of the plants that grew around them. Nowadays not so many people distinguish shapes among the green.

Plants can tell the story of how life might become tomorrow, if energy resources dwindle and supermarkets shut down. Someday we may no longer be able to count on the massive network of trucks, tractors, trains, processing centers, and monster machinery that stocks food and drugstore shelves. We are already turning to neighborhood farms and backyard gardens: sowing seeds, pulling weeds.

I guess that some people think weeds get in the way. Others ignore them. Parents often tell children that this or that is poison, don't eat it, out of ignorance, not knowledge. Poisonous plants do grow all around us. Some could kill. But distinguishable from those few grow hundreds of plants, benign and helpful, which humankind has gathered and put to use for ages.

Some seem devoted not just to ignoring this bounty but to destroying it as well. I stopped into the hardware store the other day and browsed through the herbicides, just out of curiosity. Here's a partial list, copied from two cans on the shelf, of plants guaranteed dead, thanks to the contents therein: birch, blackberry, box elder, brambles, chickweed, chicory, clover, dandelion, dock, elderberry, honeysuckle, heal-all, henbit, knotweed, lamb's quarters, mallow, mustard, oxalis, pigweed, plantain, purslane, sassafras, sheep sorrel, sumac, wild carrot, wild garlic, wild grape, wild onion, wild plum, wild radish, wild rose, wood sorrel, yarrow. The list reads like the contents of this book.

Man-made poisons have complicated the practice of gathering wild things. Herbicides, pesticides, and auto exhaust fumes damage us by damaging the soil that supports our green surroundings. If we eat plants, wild greens or cultivated vegetables, grown within their range, we might be poisoning ourselves.

Plants in cities and along automotive thoroughfares breathe deeply of lead. Their lead content decreases logarithmically with their distance from the road, and beyond one hundred feet the concentration returns to safe levels. Lead appears to coat leaves more than it seeps into roots. City greens always need washing then steaming on a rack over boiling water, which will absorb most of the remaining lead. Outside cities, railroad and power-line right-of-ways often reek of poisons too. But some produce lush greenery and fruit nonetheless, a sign of nature's unceasing fecundity. We should avoid gathering in places where we have spewed our fumes. I like instead to picture a time when berries bloom clean again.

I have a plan. We can stop poisoning and start gathering the weeds. Our bodies and our earth will live more healthfully, and we'll still keep weeds from taking over.

We gain so much from gathering wild things. Little research has pursued the nutritional value of wild plants. The few studies that exist, though, consistently prove that wild greens, particularly common weeds like dandelion, lamb's quarters, purslane, and amaranth, offer higher amounts of most vitamins and minerals than any garden vegetable gives. The wild world provides.

Wild plants have received some medical attention. Poke, may apple, and periwinkle are proving to contribute to the treatment of cancer. The cures require laboratory-extracted dosages, however; they are not home remedies. Scientific journals mention most herbal cures, if they mention them at all, as curious folk traditions. But herbs have helped heal humanity for hundreds of centuries. I can feel a cup of mint tea soothe my stomach; I feel sassafras give me a charge. But I can't explain why, nor have I found anyone else trying to explain it. Not trained in a laboratory science, I encourage others to initiate the study into the biochemical effects of herbs—not to synthesize so much as to evaluate and understand.

No one needs a scientific background to gather chicory or dandelions. Conveniently, many of the most useful plants also grow most commonly. They break through cracks in city sidewalks. I've seen lamb's quarters, purslane, mullein, amaranth, sheep sorrel and wood sorrel, chicory and dandelion in downtowns east and west. In New York City, thanks to the New York Horticultural Society, gardeners are even sowing weed seeds, hoping soon to see milkweed and wild carrot blooming in inner-city lots. Meanwhile, in suburbs, towns, and country acres, weeds keep taking over. More than half the plants in this book grow coast to coast, from southern Gulf stretches to the colder reaches of Canada. The other plants select smaller locales, but their reputations reach further.

Gail and I have tried to reflect the turn of the seasons in this book. We've marked off fifty-two chapters as if one chapter represents each week of the year. And in some climates (like our home in Virginia), that calendar should hold fairly accurately. In colder regions, winter lasts long and snows stay deep. Elsewhere, warm temperatures keep green growing all year round. Because of these latitudinal differences in season, as well as local variations from year to year, I've left out the names of the months. I'll leave it to you to note how the turning of green where you live coincides with the months of the calendar.

I conceived the outline of this book in frustration over other books about gathering wild things. Euell Gibbons's *Stalking* books (David McKay, 1962 and 1966) first captured my imagination. Lee Peterson's encyclopedic *Field Guide to Edible Wild Plants* (Houghton Mifflin, 1978) amazed me with sheer numbers of beneficial plants growing in the wild. John Lust's *The Herb Book* (Bantam, 1974) hinted at the magic of medicinal herbs. Billy Joe Tatum inspired me with clever recipes in her *Wild Foods Cookbook and Field Guide* (Workman, 1976). But I was still left wondering what I should look for when. A book that organized itself around a yearly calendar, it seemed to me, could guide people to learn about each new plant as it came ripe for gathering.

I don't think that this book solves the problem of how to identify an unknown plant found in the wild. For that, one must undergo the discipline of learning botanical terminology and follow a keyed guide like May Theilgard Watts's *Flower Finder* (Nature Study Guild, 1955), R. E. Wilkinson and H. E. Jaques's *How to Know the Weeds* (William C. Brown, 1972), Orson K. Miller, Jr.'s *Mushrooms of North America* (Dutton, 1978), or the keys in George A. Petrides's *Field Guide to Trees and Shrubs* (Houghton Mifflin, 1972) or Lauren Brown's *Weeds in Winter* (Houghton Mifflin, 1977).

But I never intended this book to be a field guide. I hope it appeals to those who keep it on the bedstand as well as those who take it out into the fields. Perhaps it will convince someone to step out more. I hope it appeals to city dwellers as well as country neighbors, to men and women, young and old. In my classes in Gathering Wild Things, I have found that an interest in useful plants can unite people with different backgrounds, politics, and lifestyles. One feels the community of humankind as it stretches into the past and into the future, supported by everlasting cycles of green growing.

Gail and I appreciate the advice and support of friends along the way. Were it not for the *Times* of Charlottesville (R.I.P.) and its staff, *Gather Ye Wild Things* might never have been concocted and the two of us might never have met. Associates and enthusiasts of the Calendar of Wild Things have kept our rewards more immediate. Members of my classes at Piedmont Virginia Community College and Wintergreen helped, whether they knew it or not, by remaining patient while I learned. Chris Hill taught me many basics of botany. Jim Schmidt helped by reading the manuscript with a scientist's eye. Nach Waxman believed in the book from the first, and his thoughtful enthusiasm helped it come to be. Rick Kot paid attention to many details in the book's production. Peter McIntosh, Teddy Crowell, Bob Vujnov, Rick

Eskin, and Jerry Porter shared our creative trials and culinary tribulations with open minds and eager bellies. Erbin Crowell fed me poke and lamb's quarters when I thought they were just weeds. The book begins with him.

And Gail and I have each other to thank as well.

Batesville, Virginia
March 1979

SPRING

Birch and Maple

T H E landscape sleeps, cold and gray. Winter lingers. Daytime breezes blow a little warmer, but nighttime frosts return. A silent spring thaw slowly tingles through the underground network. Melting snow seeps into chinks in the earth. Thirsty roots absorb the liquid, drawing it upward through the tree trunks to skies now bright, sun growing warmer day by day. The first blush of spring.

Native Americans taught European colonists to watch for spring sap runs. They practiced primitive methods of tapping, cutting a notch in the tree and thrusting a stick into it. Beneath the stick, sap dripped down and collected in a hollow log. Eventually they boiled the sap by throwing in hot rocks. Settlers continued to make the process more sophisticated. Now commercial maple producers string their sugar bushes with plastic tubing, suck out the sap with vacuum force, and boil it down over an oil furnace. But tapping trees, to catch that early spring flow, can be a simple project too.

One traditionally taps the sugar maples, but other trees run sweet as well. The sugar maple offers the greatest concentration of sweet per sap. From other maples one draws sap that simply requires a little more boiling and provides a little less syrup. Many nut trees, like the walnut and the hickory, are said to offer pleasant sap. And sweet birch sap, tapped a month later in the season, always shares that aromatic whiff of wintergreen.

I try to single out trees to tap well before the season. Each tree should measure at least a foot across. I try to recall where giant maples

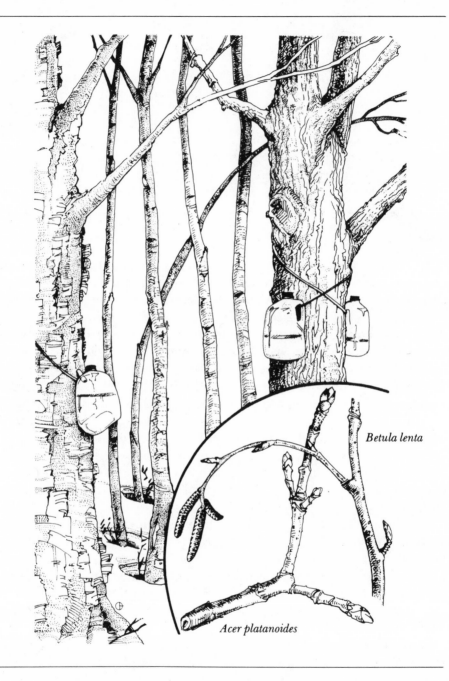

Betula lenta

Acer platanoides

spread their shady limbs last summer, verifying my memory by noticing whether twigs grow opposite one another from the branch. Few hardwoods other than maples grow in this pattern. Besides early bulging buds, opposing branches are the maple's identifying feature in the winter.

Sweet birch trees show up more conspicuously. Their iron-gray bark shows red over winter, speckled with stripes reminiscent of cherry bark. On mature trunks, large flakes of bark curl off. Up above, hanging catkins winter over; ready to drop seed. Pinch off a twig to be sure you've found sweet birch: note the fragrance, like pungent wintergreen.

Taps go into maples at the first sign of warming weather. Morning sunshine brings gallons of water heaving upward from underground, moving toward leaf and flower buds atop the trees. Nighttime freezes send the water down again. In the midst of this spring initiative, we borrow some of the flow. The sap that rises first carries an abundance of minerals, so taps should be there to catch it as early as January or February in the northwest and south, as late as April in the midwest and northeast. New England farmers sense the timing in their bones.

Sap travels through the trees in the xylem layer, one to three inches beneath the bark. Use a brace and bit to drill a hole: waist high, about two inches deep, angling slightly upward. Some say that taps on the southern, sun-soaked side of trees flow more abundantly. Tapholes should match the width of your spiles, as the tapping spouts are called. Sumac or elderberry bushes provide fine natural spiles. Cut a stalk to a length of four or five inches and hollow it out with a circular file or knife. Oldtimers catch the drip in covered buckets, but plastic gallon jugs fit fine. Cut a hole near the handle for your spile to enter. Loop a rope through the handle and around the trunk of the tree to secure the jug against the weight of the sap. A good flow yields more than a gallon a day—small measure, compared to the hundred to two hundred fifty gallons shot up through the tree each springtime day.

Sweet sap ferments easily, so jugs must be emptied every day. I suggest you freeze the sap as you collect it, not only for safe storage, but as the first step in an easy condensation process. Boiling sap takes time and special equipment, and makes more steam than most kitchens can bear. From every forty to sixty gallons of sap you draw, you'll extract one gallon of syrup. That means thirty-nine to fifty-nine gallons of water rising as steam, if you boil the sap. But try freezing it instead.

Let a jug of frozen sap thaw until it is about one-third liquid, surrounding a hard core of ice. The sugar solution melts more quickly, while pure water stays ice. Pour off the liquid, then freeze it again and repeat the thawing and draining process. Once you have condensed the gathered sap to a manageable amount, you can finish it off over a kitchen burner, simmering it to the syrupy consistency you like. Syrup's done when it sheets off a spoon. Beware not to burn it.

Maple sap makes syrup, but birch sap makes beer. These trees take a tap about a month later than the maples, when spring is in full swing. You need a lot less birch sap to make a good batch of brew, since it need not undergo condensation. You can begin with as little as three gallons of birch sap, less than a week's flow. Toss in two quarts of sweet birch twig ends and bark shavings. Simmer them in the sap for half an hour. Sweet aromas fill the air. Strain the liquid, then add five pounds of sugar and a package of dry yeast. Cover the concoction in a crock and let it sit three weeks. It will bubble and brew. Skim and strain the potion, then siphon into bottles. Add half a teaspoon of sugar to each bottle you fill, cap each tightly, and wait a few weeks before you taste.

Even if you forgo birch beer this year, you can brew a simple cup of sweet birch tea any time of the year. Toss those twig ends and bark shavings into a pot of boiling water and simmer for half an hour. That clean wintergreen aroma pervades your home. The tea is sweet and soothing. From the bark of sweet birch and the leaves of wintergreen pharmacists distill methyl salicylate, a natural forerunner to today's aspirin, still occasionally used as a liniment rub.

Current research suggests that sweet birch sweetness will not cause cavities. In fact it may even protect against them. The commercial sugar substitute xylitol comes originally from the sweet birch tree, and some say it even reverses the development of tooth decay. Debates continue on the issue, but I still chew a sprig of sweet birch whenever I find it, using a blunt twig as toothbrush, floss, and toothpick from the wild.

Catch the sap of an awakening birch or maple: it's an omen of a good year to come. Abundant flows reward timely efforts, in harmony with cycles of the wild. The wild world begins to open, sharing its sweet secrets. Spring's beginning, and you're ready.

Wild Easter Eggs

EASTER rites reach back centuries before Jesus to pagan times, when women and men sang songs of spring's awakening. Undertones of primitive celebration still harmonize within the hymns of Christ's rebirth, and we still follow the changing cycles of nature as we set the date for Easter: the first Sunday after the full moon once the sun has entered Aries. Even the name summons up the shadow of Eostre, long-forgotten Anglo-Saxon goddess of spring and the dawn. Her believers must have celebrated her presence around the vernal equinox, as the full moon set and the new dawn came forth shining.

Imagine an Easter basket created in memory of that ancient goddess. Flesh-colored eggs, pink, white, and brown, fresh laid this morning. Wildflowers trim the eggs with fragile colors from the woodland spring. Eggs symbolize the unborn, flowers symbolize a new beginning, and they mingle in a nest of new-grown grass or hay, like the earth that sustains us. An Easter basket can renew the earthly origins of our traditional springtime fest.

Pressed flowers, picked this spring or last, decorate Easter eggs elegantly. If nature's spring precedes Easter this year, colorful flowers bloom in abundance. Place small blooms—violets, periwinkles, fruit blossoms especially—between sheets of wax paper. Cushion them in sheets of newspaper, then press them flat with heavy books or other

heavy objects. A week's pressing will do, leaving the flowers flat but not brittle.

If nature's spring is far behind this year, perhaps you left flowers from last year's bounty in a book somewhere, a forgotten spring souvenir. Flowers pressed for more than a month tend to stay flat, refusing to bend with the curve of the egg. Try soaking them in a dish of warm water for five or ten minutes before using them. Use plain white glue, like Elmer's, to attach pressed flowers to the curve of an egg. You can cover the flowers with glue too, since it dries clear and leaves a protective coating.

Even if no flowers bloom and no other greens are showing, evergreen ferns and fir boughs still provide ornamental leaves. But most evergreen leaves are too bulky to fit the delicate curve of an egg.

Better to use them under onionskin egg dyes. Wrap a raw egg, covering it completely with stray skins of onions, brown or red. Tuck green fronds between skins and shell to make a silhouette. Tie the wrapped egg tightly with cheesecloth and drop it into boiling water for twelve minutes. Remove it from water, let it cool, unwrap it, and *voilà!* a pleasing marbled texture: an earthy, naturally dyed Eostre egg. Experiment by adding your pressed springtime blossoms beneath the layer of onionskins. New shapes and colors will emerge on the egg's surface.

Directions for the perfect Eostre basket, simply woven from honeysuckle vines, appear in Leslie Linsley's *Wildcrafts* (Doubleday, 1977). Fill it with fresh wild flowers and eggs naturally dyed to revive the ancient spring. Modern Easter celebrations seem strangely disjointed: what has a chocolate-marshmallow bunny rabbit to do with nature's rebirth? In the flowers of springtime we unite the rites of old and the modern-day meaning of Easter. Rebirth blossoms every spring.

Redbud and Violet

A FAINT green mist hangs in the treetops. Then redbud darts into bloom, mauve blossoms on stark black boughs. The petals are pastel but seem shocking amidst gray shadows of winter lingering in the woods.

The eastern redbud tree may stand up to fifty feet tall, squeezed thin in wooded areas but spreading broad when given space. Its range extends from the central Atlantic coastline into the Midwest. A shrubby cousin grows in California and a larger western redbud graces

Texas and New Mexico. All redbuds flower bright and early, before their leaves arrive.

A branch of redbud offers pleasure to many senses. Clusters of lavender flowers dangle from dark twigs, which curve like Oriental brush strokes. You sense its odor in the air. Draw closer and taste a single bloom, penetrating its inner center of sweetness. That flavor, subtle as spring's morning light, can adorn this season's menu.

I like to pluck a handful of blossoms and toss them over a spring salad. That corner of the dining table begins to resemble the woods outside. Redbud's cheery color brightens white desserts like custard or rice pudding: just stir in a handful of blossoms before you set the dish in the oven to bake. And homemade ice cream can be infused with the pastel color and flavor of early redbud blooms.

Where the redbuds bloom too high, beyond my reach, I console myself with violets. Their familiar flowers open in lawns, fields, and forests early in the spring, shy companions to the redbud blooms above. Sometimes violets grow so abundantly that they wash a lawn in blues that mirror the sky overhead.

More than one hundred species of violet grow in the United States and Canada, from the tiny white field pansy to the round-leafed yellow violet to the birdfoot, with purple flowers and intricate leaves shaped to match its name. Most familiar is the common blue violet *(Viola papilionacea)*, with heart-shaped leaves and delicate purple flowers. Every violet signals spring; all add festive color and nutritional value to springtime meals.

Gardeners over the years have cultivated violets for color and fragrance, appreciating, too, the deep green foliage offered by the plant from spring to fall. Few have known that the humble violet offers healthy salad greens as well. Euell Gibbons's experiments proved that half a cup of violet leaves provides almost twice the adult daily requirement of vitamin A—more, perhaps, than one should eat at once. Leaves and flowers provide substantial amounts of vitamin C as well.

Violets have long been prized for their medicinal properties. Many an old herbal prescribes violet blossom syrup for coughs and colds; the vitamin content, if nothing else, would help the ailment. Violet leaves

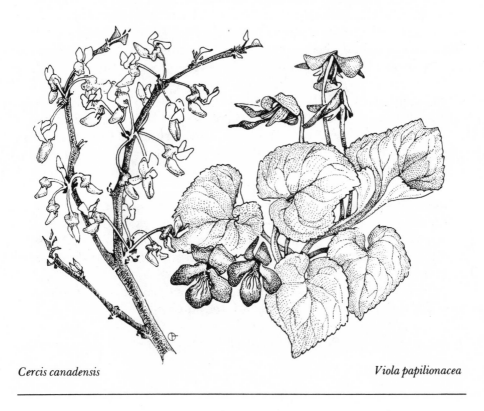

Cercis canadensis   *Viola papilionacea*

act as a gentle laxative if eaten about a quarter cup at a time. Even violet roots have been collected and prepared as an expectorant remedy for coughs and bronchitis.

Many people prefer to indulge in violet sweets, either jelly or candied blossoms. The recipes are simple, although the gathering takes time. But time spent among the violets feels like heaven: quiet, serene, spring forever. Preserved violets will hint at that feeling throughout the year.

For violet jelly, gather a fully-packed quart of dry, open blossoms. Pour boiling water over them and let the infusion sit for one to twelve hours (the longer period if you plan to strain out the flowers). Add the juice of one lemon, and blue violet turns toward rose-red. Use this infusion and follow any standard jelly recipe provided with commercial pectin. Add two to four cups of sugar, depending on your taste. Bring to a boil, add pectin, boil further, jar, and seal. Many recipes for violet jelly call for you to strain the flowers from the infusion, but then you will miss the pleasure of flowers floating on your breakfast muffin. If your jelly doesn't jell, you still have rich violet syrup, which can be used on hot cakes and waffles, ice cream, yogurt, and in herbal teas.

For candied violets, pick flowers with the stems attached. Beat an egg white lightly, just until it froths. Dip each flower in egg white, then dip it in a bowl of extra-fine granulated sugar. You might want to use a small paintbrush for touch-ups. It is important to get every bit of the flower coated in sugar to preserve it. Let the coated flowers dry on wax paper—it may take a few days—then store them between layers of wax paper in a tight tin or plastic container in the refrigerator or freezer. Many use candied violets for special cake decorations, and there must be many other uses for these floral delicacies.

Spring abounds in flowers. Springtime meals can abound in flowers too. The pale pinks and purples of redbud and violet blossoms can adorn salads and sweets, cheering the eye and palate. And, with a little preparation, spring flowers bloom on the pantry shelf all year round.

Wild Garden Before the Plough

A GARDEN left dormant over winter often hides wild treasure. Among those ragged remains, tender seedlings emerge. Hidden roots send up spring greens. Before you turn the soil to plant seeds for a deliberate garden, take a look at what nature has tossed into your garden plot.

A starburst of green leaves tinged red by winter's frost lies close to the ground. Underneath, a white root, also touched with red, reaches several inches into the soil. A wild radish grows in your garden. The winter presence of a year-old evening primrose plant *(Oenothera biennis)*, this radish tastes sweet raw or cooked. It tingles in your mouth, but never gets as hot as a table radish. Scrub it, then slice it into spring salads if you like the taste.

If you leave it to grow in your garden summer long, your wild radish will send up a flower stalk almost two feet high by fall. The fragrant yellow evening primrose flowers will bloom in late summer, and they are sweet to the taste as well. I just nibble them whenever I find them, but you could use them as a salad or pickle garnish too. The roots of the evening primrose have been eaten by native Americans for centuries.

Alongside the wild radish may be scattered the new leaves of wild carrots. Dig deep under the soil, down around the root supporting this feathery foliage, and you can pull out a tough white wild carrot. A whiff of the root reminds you of the cultivated kind.

The wild carrot (unlike the wild radish) is a close relative of the garden vegetable. If you let your cultivated carrots go to seed their second year, their flowers will resemble the well-known Queen Anne's lace. And indeed "wild carrot" is just another name for Queen Anne's lace, that familiar summer wildflower growing abundantly throughout the United States and Canada.

Be careful though. There are several dangerously poisonous plants resembling the wild carrot, although they grow much less abundantly than their edible relative and generally prefer a soggier environment. A cautious forager checks for five signs that distinguish the wild carrot from poison hemlock, water hemlock, and fool's parsley. Number one: a cluster of tubular roots, rather than a single slender taproot, signals danger: water hemlock. Number two: tall carrot- or parsley-like plants, over the three-foot height to which wild carrot grows, may be dangerous poison or water hemlock. Number three: any such plant that exudes a musky odor could be fool's parsley or poison hemlock. Number four: purple stripes or blotches on a smooth stalk characterize the poison hemlock. Wild carrot stalks grow green and fuzzy. And finally, number five: only the aging wild carrot flowerhead curls up

Oenothera biennis

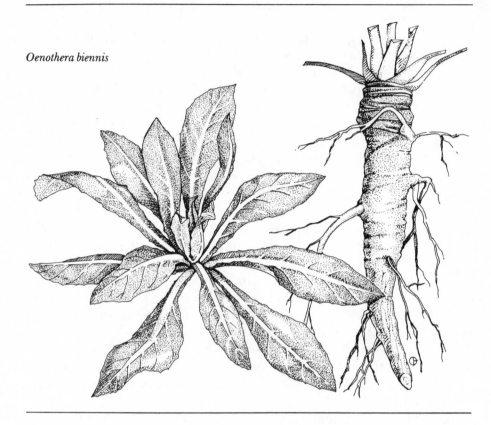

cuplike around the mature seed stock. The seedheads of fool's parsley, poison and water hemlock stay flat open like umbrellas as they dry. If you memorize these few details, you can pull up wild carrots without a worry.

Although they may be quite tough, wild carrot roots are edible raw. They can be boiled for a vegetable dish or used raw as a garnish. Many people enjoy the greens chopped into a salad. Even the seeds, gathered in fall, winter, and early spring, taste good. They have a delicate anise taste that seems to intensify through the winter. Hang fully-formed seedheads upside down to dry, if you want to store these spicy wild things.

Along with wild radishes and carrots, your garden may be growing wild broccoli too, as Euell Gibbons calls the flowering stage of the wintercress. This plant offers tasty greens when others have succumbed to cold (see "Winter Greens"). Now, as spring flowers sense the sunshine, wintercress comes into full bloom. Once the flower buds form, but before they open out in yellow petals, wintercress spears can be cooked for a tender vegetable dish. Bring a potful of wild broccoli and water to a boil; after five minutes, discard the water and add fresh. Bring it just to a boil once more, then serve wild broccoli spears with melted butter or cheese sauce.

Doubtless many other wild things will have crept into your garden this spring, and many will persist all summer, no matter how carefully you hoe and mulch and weed. Once you begin to recognize sprouting lamb's quarters, chickweed, purslane, sorrel, amaranth, and others, you may feel yourself slipping free of the ever-pressing need to weed, weed, weed. Instead of stripping the earth bare of every plant that chose to grow there, why not share your garden with the wild? Too many of these plants, of course, become unwelcome intruders. But even those you choose to uproot can go right into the kitchen or the compost.

Weeds can actually help your garden grow. Some, for example, serve as indicators of soil conditions. If tart, lemony sorrels abound in your garden, the soil is probably acidic: lime or wood ash should be added to make the best growing environment. Many weeds (dandelion and chicory, for instance) grow deep, tapping the earth's underground reserve of minerals. When they die and decompose, they leave those minerals at the surface of the earth, to be used by other plants around them. Pulled weeds, put into the compost, replenish the earth in which your vegetables grow. Other weeds keep your garden pest-free with insect-repellent aromas (see "Wild Herbs in the Garden"). And, if my few claims don't convince you, try to find a copy of J. Cocannouer's book *Weeds, Guardians of the Soil* (Devin-Adair, 1950).

Probably the wisest plan is to weed selectively. Don't pull out something just because you didn't plant it. Learn to recognize the weeds in your garden and try to discover what they offer. The truth of the matter is that, given all the wild things that can be picked for eating, an untended garden may provide as much nutritious food as a carefully weeded one. For most people this would be going a bit too far, but gardens and weeds certainly need not be enemies. With your help, they can live together in harmony.

Spring Shoots

SPRING warmth eases sprouts out of underground hiding. With each rain new plants appear, many tender, many edible. And among the spring sprouts asparagus reigns, a gourmet delicacy from the wild.

Asparagus thrives in fields and pastures and along roadsides and railway rights-of-way throughout the East and Midwest. It may also be found in moist areas west to the coast. Each spring, sturdy sprouts shove up through the confusion of grass and leaves. The skeletons of last year's asparagus bushes, bleached and mangled by winter, may help you locate this year's sprouts. Look for the thick white stems and the auxiliary branches growing at right angles from the stalks. Sometimes a full stand of last year's asparagus will remain, feathery foliage still clinging to thick central trunks. Once spring rains soak their perennial root systems, short fat shoots begin to poke through the rubble.

Asparagus sprouts are delectable as long as they are still tender enough to snap off. If left to grow, they mature quickly into tough green stalks. Young leaves cling tightly to a spear, hiding the promise of a branch set to spread out long, thin, and horizontal. When sprouts go undiscovered, these branches soon harden and bloom yellow bell flowers. By late summer full-grown asparagus bushes bedeck the fields like Christmas trees. Their boughs bear bright red seed pods on into winter.

Asparagus came to this continent as a cultivated vegetable, quaintly called "sparrowgrass" by English here and back home. The plant went wild long ago, its seeds carried off by birds and wind, to spring up randomly across the landscape. Now many country folk, as part of their rites of spring, count on finding wild asparagus. Some mark the locations of hardy plants, returning to the same spots several times a season, year after year. The plant wants to set seed, so for each sprout

Asparagus officinalis

that is pulled another quickly emerges, until finally the asparagus jumps into bloom before anyone can trim it back.

Since wild asparagus is identical to the cultivated variety, recipes for cooking it are not scarce. Steamed fresh spears are simplest. Top with grated white cheese and sesame seeds for the last three minutes of steaming, and you've made an elegant wild lunch. Briefly blanched wild asparagus spears freeze well too. The wild spears are often so much more tender than those bought in the store—so tender I like to snip them raw into a salad. And even as secondary branches unfold, I snip the tender tips.

Wild asparagus has performed a service far beyond its role as a tasty springtime vegetable. Thanks to Euell Gibbons, wild asparagus stalks have opened up the world of gathering wild things for many. Millions know of him and the plant that made him famous. Millions have absorbed, if only from his first book's catchy title, the pleasing lessons that he offered in *Stalking the Wild Asparagus*. Tasty enough to convince the most skeptical palate, wild asparagus became the fitting symbol of what Euell Gibbons had to tell us: the finest of vegetable delicacies grow wild and free all around us.

Sassafras

SASSAFRAS is more American than apple pie. Recognized by Europeans as one of the most distinctive plants this wild new world would offer, sassafras raised political and economic issues within the first years of colonial settlement. It has provoked controversy as far back as its recorded history goes, and it continues to provoke controversy today. But, long before the European settlement, sassafras was gathered by natives of this continent, who knew its sweet, spicy flavor as one of their own.

Every part of the tree beckons with a distinctive smell. Even in winter, a twig snapped off declares a sassafras flavor. Come spring, green begins to glow in the treetops. Soon miniature leaves emerge, accompanied by clustering yellow flowers, spicy-fragrant to the smell. The leaves mature to show their three characteristic shapes, often all on a single tree: the oval, the mitten, and the fleur-de-lis. Leaves, too, exude a fragrance. I can't resist nibbling new sassafras leaves like a goat.

Yet the most potent part of the sassafras remains unseen. From sassafras root bark comes that flavor we all reminisce about. It reminds us of old-time root beer, whether we ever drank it or not. Unearth a young sassafras seedling, and take a whiff of the root's bark. Often it will curl right off the woody portion of the root. You can smell it the moment it hits the air.

Perhaps colonists became excited over this American native because they found Indians putting it to so many uses. Wherever sassafras grew, Indians gathered and used it—as a tea to treat measles, as medication against bowel and bladder pains, as a spring tonic to thin the blood, as a flavorful smoke. Settlers shipped the roots back to their homelands with claims that sassafras could be used against pests, fevers, baldness, broken bones, and to improve one's health and spirits. When sassafras gained a reputation for curing venereal diseases, debate raged even hotter over whether it was a proper crop on which to found a nation. The far-reaching claims for sassafras's medicinal powers may not have been all colonial P.R. Modern herbals classify sassafras as an anodyne and an antiseptic, suggesting that the tea made of the root bark will alleviate pain and cleanse infections.

While every portion of the sassafras tree has its uses, foragers have always considered the root bark the most precious, brewing it into a spring tea. Spring is a good time to gather roots, before they have sent their secret upward into limbs and leaves. Sassafras tea lends a punch to anyone who wants to start off the season with gusto. A natural stimulant, it really does feel like it gets spring blood flowing.

To make sassafras tea, I try to find slender saplings whose roots will be slim and flexible. About three inches underground, thin rootlets are to be found, usually extending outward in opposite directions. If roots are an inch or less in diameter I don't bother to detach the bark, for the wood is tender and will not affect the taste of the tea. Once we came across a large sassafras trunk upturned. From it we could shave off root bark that grew half an inch thick.

Before a tea can be brewed, dirt must be scrubbed off the root parts. With clippers or a hatchet, I break each root into conveniently short lengths so that they will fit into a pot on the stove. A good handful—say seven to ten lengths of sassafras root—will brew up a good quart or two of tea. Toss in the roots, then bring the pot of water

Sassafras albidum

to a boil. Let it boil gently about half an hour. The color will turn dramatically from thin brown to deep woodland red. That color is a good indicator that the tea is done. The same handful of root twigs will brew several batches of tea. Just pour in another quart of water and repeat the boiling process.

From this sassafras tea, one can also make an exotic wild spice jelly. Sometimes I add sweet birch and wild allspice twigs or wild ginger roots to ornament the flavor. Make a strong tea, then use it as the base for a simple jelly recipe. For each cup of tea, add a cup of sugar or half a cup of honey. Bring to a boil, then add powdered pectin, boil a minute, then spoon into sterile jars. The color is woodsy and the flavor divine.

Sassafras is making news again. This time the controversy surrounds safrole, a key ingredient of sassafras found also in nutmeg and mace. Oil of sassafras contains eighty percent safrole, while sassafras tea contains four to ten parts per million. Laboratory experiments have shown that animals fed large, steady doses of safrole over several years develop severe liver cancer. One researcher describes safrole as a "weak carcinogen which requires prolonged insult to a biologic system before manifesting cellular changes."

Government officials felt that these results warranted the prohibition of safrole in food on the market. In 1976 the Food and Drug Commissioner more directly specified that any food containing safrole or oil of sassafras—he names sassafras bark sold to brew tea as his example—is "deemed to be adulterated" and "cannot be lawfully marketed in interstate commerce."

Herb traders, incensed at government intrusion into their business, have come up with a few answers to these test results. Safrole, particularly synthetic safrole, may indeed cause liver cancer, says Ben Zaricor of the Fmali Herb Company. But no one, he points out, ingests pure safrole and, besides, it may affect the body differently when it is an integral part of home-brewed sassafras tea.

The debates continue. The last major sassafras case to be brought before the courts died before its conclusion, since the evidentiary root lost its potency before the case was argued. Sassafras root is by law an illegal commodity, yet some herb dealers still sell it. And many people still go out in search of sassafras spring tonic at this time of year, as I do, presuming that an outing in the spring air and a tea made from the roots of the earth can only improve one's health and spirits.

Cleavers

SPRING weeds establish themselves in backyards, fields, and forests, growing ever more lush and unavoidable. Among them grows cleavers, a trailing, lowdown weed, easily overlooked and easily forgotten. Its ribbed, sticky stalk holds a whorl of six or eight slender, sticky leaves. After a month of inconspicuous growth in early spring, it puts out minuscule white flowers, which dot the leaf clusters. In another month, by early summer, cleavers completes its cycle, producing joined pairs of green, sticky fruits about the size of a peppercorn.

When cleavers is seen under a magnifying glass, its stickiness turns out to be the effect of many crooked hairs extending a fraction of an inch above leaf and stalk surfaces. These hairs are essential to cleavers's survival. The plant's stalks grow a foot to three feet long but they can't stand upright on their own. They depend on the support of neighbor weeds, cleaving to leaves and grass around them as they reach for the sun. Seeds cling too, so that every passing dog and cat, horse and cow, sock and pantleg carries cleavers away. No wonder cleavers grows abundantly throughout the North American continent.

In Europe, where cleavers probably originated, it gained a reputation as a healing herb. A strong tea made of its leaves and stems was used inside and outside the body. A cup of cleavers tea was thought to cure scurvy, urinary ailments, colds, and insomnia. Applied externally, tradition claims, it relieved cuts, scrapes, and skin irritations. Cleavers tea has been valued as a complexion treatment too, healing acne and sunburn, and even lightening freckles. The herb is diuretic as well. This property earned for cleavers its American folk reputation as a plant for dieters to eat or drink as tea.

Since cleavers is so widespread, and because it is safe, we may as well begin to use it. To eat cleavers, you have to find your way past its hairy texture and get down to the healthy green taste. You can chop it

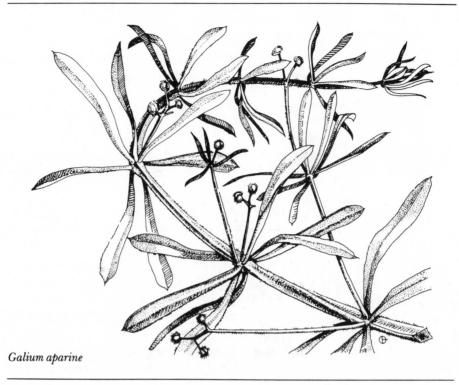

Galium aparine

fine into your next tossed salad or steam it thoroughly. Its fuzz will fade. Or you can avoid the plant's sticky problems by steeping it as a tea. Harvest blossoming stalks and hang them upside down for two to four weeks in a dark, dry place. Steep a tea as usual, pouring a cup of boiling water over each one or two teaspoons of the dried herb, leaves, stems, flowers, and all. Cleavers tea tastes mildly green, good enough to store for winter brews.

Some people even have the patience to collect cleavers's minuscule seed pods and roast them slowly until they turn brown for a wild and gentle coffee substitute. Lay seeds on a cooking sheet and bake them gently at about 200 degrees F. (95 degrees C.) until their color changes and you begin to smell their sweet roast flavor—about an hour. Cleavers and coffee, in fact, are botanically related, both belonging to the order Rubiaceae.

It seems ironic that such a useful plant should proliferate unseen, considered a pest if considered at all. But, once you recognize cleavers for what it is, it pops up everywhere. Appreciation almost seems to increase the yield of this modest plant of hidden virtues.

Sorrels

G OURMET chefs know sorrel as a French cooking herb, the basis for fine soups and fish sauces. On this side of the ocean, French sorrel grows in tended gardens only. But gatherers in the wild know other sorrels as common wayside weeds, easy to find and pleasing to the taste. While the plants we group under the heading "sorrels" are not all botanically related, they share the acidic quality from which their name (taken from the German for "sour") derives. All thrive in spring and summer, some making it through mild winters too. All offer reliable greens for salads, seasoning, and thirst-quenching drinks.

Sheep sorrel, wild counterpart to the revered French herb, clusters in clearings, gardens, backyards, and fields across the North American continent. Its shallow red roots support bunches of arrowhead leaves, and from among these grow spikes of reddening flowers, lifting upward to six inches tall. Leaves and flowers share the characteristic tangy taste, but choicest among the parts are the large leaves that unfold before the plant sets flower. Similar in shape and taste to the cooking herb, the smaller leaves of sheep sorrel can be substituted for the fancy stuff in any gourmet recipe.

Garden sorrel, a closer cousin to French sorrel, grows in eastern Canada, ranging south into New England and Pennsylvania. This species looks similar to sheep sorrel but larger. Its roots dig deeper, its

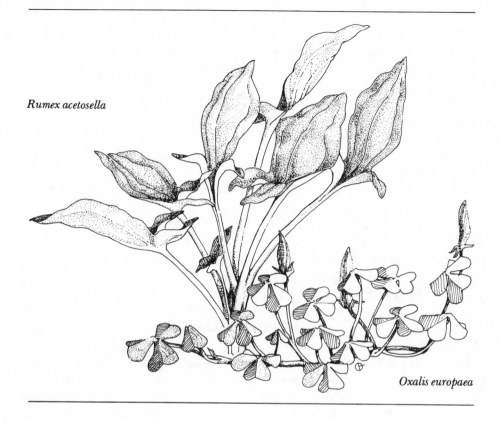

Rumex acetosella

Oxalis europaea

stem grows more stout, and its leaves spread more broadly than those of the more common sheep sorrel. Both sheep sorrel and garden sorrel were no doubt brought across the ocean by early colonists. But sheep sorrel has traveled coast to coast, while garden sorrel's growth pattern remains localized.

From Canada to Mexico and everywhere in between, a third sorrel thrives. Wood sorrel—perhaps misleadingly named—shares nothing but its acidic qualities with the sheep and garden sorrels. It pokes around in cities and towns, backyards and roadsides, as well as woods and abandoned pastures. Many know wood sorrel as "trefoil" or "shamrock," and it is sometimes confused with clover because of its three-leaf shape. From its small taproot spring branching clusters of three delicate heart-shaped leaves. Dainty yellow or lavender flowers bloom in summer heat and pickle-shaped seedpods grow with the season. Its leaves, flowers, and fruits taste tart. Children know this friendly weed even when adults don't.

Once you have identified any of the sorrels growing in your neighborhood, you can put them to good use. As long as I have them to gather, I include sorrels in hot and cold teas. A summer drink made from a hefty handful of fresh sorrel leaves, steeped for ten minutes then strained and iced, can taste better than lemonade or lipton's. Sorrel leaves, whatever the species, sprinkled over your salad greens add crisp, green, tangy flavor and pretty shapes to the salad bowl. Used in cooking, sorrels can go either way: vegetative or dessertified.

One of my favorite early summer treats is Green Tomatoes Dressed with Wood Sorrel. Cut green tomatoes into thin slices and dip them into a batter made of ¼ cup cornmeal, 1 beaten egg, and ¼ teaspoon each salt and basil. Add water if the batter seems thick. Fry the tomatoes in butter, turn them once and reduce the heat. Scatter over them a layer of pretty trefoil leaves. Grate white cheese over them, then scatter more leaves on top. You can make this dish as a casserole by layering the tomatoes, sorrel, and cheese alternately. Let it simmer or bake slowly for about fifteen minutes before serving.

That's sorrel as a vegetable. Here's sorrel for dessert. For a simple sweet, try a Tart Wood Sorrel Cake. Combine ¾ cup unbleached white flour, ¾ cup whole grain flour, ¼ cup wheat germ, 2 teaspoons baking powder, and ½ teaspoon salt. Into these dry ingredients stir ⅓ cup soft butter, ½ cup sorghum molasses or honey, and ⅔ cup milk. Beat the batter for a minute. Then add an egg and ⅓ cup fruit juice and beat another minute. Fold in ½ cup wood sorrel leaves, flowers, and seedpods. Bake the batter in a greased cake pan for about an hour at 350° F. If you ice the cake with a light frosting, you can trim it with more trefoils.

So versatile and ubiquitous are the sorrels, they quickly become a regular addition to many a meal. They garnish a plate or give salads a little zing. They make a substantial addition to broth or cream soups. They brew a refreshing tea. They come in spring and they last all summer, so you have months in which to get to know the sorrels growing around you.

In Defense of Dandelions

L o the poor dandelion, villainized over the years, considered by most a despicable weed. Tons of dandelion killer are dumped on lawns every year, and special instruments have been invented just to wrench the sturdy plant from its abode. Judging from the literature, for each scientist studying the virtues of this common plant, ten others are developing ever more potent poisons to kill it.

Life wasn't always so hard for the dandelion. The plant's botanical name, *Taraxacum officinale*, reveals that for eighteenth-century Europe the dandelion offered the "official remedy for disorders." Dandelion roots and greens are known to have been used in a spring tonic as far back as A.D. 1000. For centuries before the present-day obsession with clean-clipped lawns, dandelion blooms represented good health and renewed vigor.

The age-old effectiveness of dandelion spring tonics can now be ascribed to the plant's remarkably high vitamin and mineral content. Newgrown dandelions provide 14,000 milligrams of vitamin A per 100 grams of greens, according to Euell Gibbons's figures. That means that one-half cup of fresh spring greens gives almost five times the minimum adult daily requirement of vitamin A—more than one would want to eat at one sitting, since too much vitamin A can be toxic. These greens also provide almost half the daily requirement of vitamin C. The dandelion plant abounds in minerals and other vitamins as well: thiamine, riboflavin, calcium, sodium, and potassium all collect in its roots. Even if you don't care about tapping this resource for yourself, remember that the soil in which a dandelion grows could use its earthy riches. Compost the dandelions you pull; every plant tossed into a plastic garbage bag or eradicated with poison depletes the soil of minerals it contributed to the plant in the first place.

Almost every part of the dandelion, from root to blossom, is edible. The roots are most often scrubbed, roasted, and ground to make a

Taraxacum officinale

coffee substitute or addition, as are the roots of chicory (see further instructions in "Chicory"). Dandelion roots will be most substantial if they are pulled before the plant blooms or after it has shed its seeds. Small tender roots can also be scrubbed, sliced, and boiled like carrots for a dinner vegetable.

Just above the root, the crown is sweet and tender too. Pull up a dandelion by the root and you will find this silky-white ground-level section where root meets greens. Sliced raw or cooked, dandelion crowns enhance a salad. Deep within the crowns sleep unborn buds, the promise of dandelion flowers. These little nubs, if you can collect enough, make a tasty cooked vegetable or garnish for an omelet. And once they ascend on stems into the open air, the sweet dandelion buds provide a delicious and nutritious cooked vegetable dish.

For tasty greens, try to find dandelions before they begin to bloom. Long, jagged leaves grow from a single center. Long ago this leaf shape inspired the plant's name. Someone thought they looked like fangs and named the plant *dent de lion:* tooth of the lion. A sturdy central vein and milky sap further characterize the spring dandelion.

Once they bloom, the flowers taste good too. As with so many other wild things, the blooming dandelion flower claims strength and sugar from the rest of the plant. Roots grow stringy, leaves bitter and tough, when flowers open in the late spring and summer sunshine.

Luxurious dandelion blossoms reflect the glowing sun as it urges them open day by day. Children love their color, but most adults have to make an effort to love them all over again. A few simple recipes may convince you that these sunny flowers can brighten springtime menus.

Fried dandelion blossoms come as a surprising treat to many. Pick fully opened blooms, being sure not to get a bit of the bitter stem. Dip the flowers in a simple batter: 1 cup milk plus 1 egg, beaten together, plus 1 cup flour plus ½ teaspoon each baking powder and salt. Fry the dipped blooms in hot oil over medium heat. Sweet golden hors d'oeuvres.

Squeamish guests may have trouble devouring dandelion blossoms, but no one will question dandelion wine. Many recipes exist; here is one from my friend Bertha Ross. She makes a rich, sweet wine which ages magnificently to a bourbon-brown color. One afternoon Bertha treated me to a glass of dandelion wine that she had kept in her cupboard for eight years. It tasted like exquisite sherry and it brought on the smiles. Here's her recipe. Increase quantities in the recipe according to how many dandelion blossoms you gather.

To 1 gallon of blossoms, add sections of 2 unpeeled lemons, 2 unpeeled oranges, 2 peeled grapefruits, and a cup of raisins. Add about 1 cup of sugar. Cover all with boiling water and stir well. When the mixture has cooled to lukewarm, stir in a package of dry baking yeast. Let this potion sit, well covered, for a week. Stir it at least once a day.

Now strain out the fruits and flowers. Be sure to wring handfuls of the flowers through cheesecloth so you get every drop of liquid that you can. Strain it once more through wet cheesecloth. Add about 4 pounds of sugar, more depending on your taste. Bertha sips the potion at this point and usually adds more sugar than I would—but it always comes out tasting right. The dandelions' bitterness needs special compensation.

Let the sweetened wine sit for another five days. Then bottle it in jars with screw-on lids, but don't seal the bottles tightly. Wait until fermentation ceases—about three weeks—and you no longer hear the bubbles rising. The longer you wait to break into this sunshine brew, the better it will taste. Sometimes Bertha even waits until dandelions bloom again for her first sip of a new brew.

The special taste of dandelion wine should be enough to coax even the fanatic lawn trimmer into using the flowers. Sure, go ahead, pull the roots up—even use that fancy gadget—but roast the roots you gather into a warm morning brew. Fine, clip off those flowers before they go to seed. But blend those blossoms into a wine of fine bouquet. Use the dandelion parts you want, and return the rest of the plant to earth as compost. Weed your lawn, feed your soil, and feed yourself. Three cheers for the lowly dandelion.

Poke

BLEACHED, jagged skeletons sprawl on the ground. They must have stood six feet tall when they were growing. Here and there the remains of a berry cluster nestle into mulch. Poke seeds scatter. A few to the birds, a few to the deer, a few to the ground, perhaps to germinate. Thick perennial taproots persist underground.

Once the weather's warm, poke sprouts. Papery leaves clasp a fat stalk. From this delicate beginning emerges the full-grown plant, standing tall as a woman, arms stretched out, laden heavy with blue berries.

Those who have lived with the land wherever pokeweed grows (from Maine, Ontario, Minnesota southward) have recognized its powers. Native American tribes throughout the area each held beliefs about poke's curative powers. They recognized that its virtue dwelt in its root. Some used the root as a poultice on sores and skin ailments. Others laid fresh root on hands and feet: a fever cure. Some took the root internally, but with great caution, for tradition warned of its poison.

White settlers moved in and stayed, country people. Like the Indians, they took to eating early sprouts of poke. Poke salad, as country people still call it, means the cooked young greens. They learned (from tradition, taste, and experience) to cook poke in two changes of water and never to eat it raw. The poison that lingers in the roots year round travels upward as the plant begins to flower. Stems and leaves change in texture, becoming distasteful as the plant matures. I scout out poke as early as I can find it and check every stalk over about eight inches tall once the leaves begin to unfurl. I leave behind any sprouts that show a sign of flowering curled within their endmost leaves.

Poke sprouts when spring can't turn back to winter anymore. The sun shines down too warmly; plenty of rain has soaked the ground. I look around the ghostly stalks of last year's plants for a sign of green life at the base. Day-old nubs are the most delectable. Cut off sprouts above the ground. You'll need a knife and a bag or basket in which to carry home plenty, since poke cooks down.

By blanching young shoots briefly (one to three minutes), either in boiling water or over steam, you coax most of the bitterness out of the herb and into the water, which will turn bright red. Continue to use the once-cooked poke sprouts as if they were a raw vegetable. To eat them plain, bring them once more to a quick boil in fresh water, then serve with butter, vinegar, sour cream, or grated cheese. I often cook them for the second time in a frypan with garlic, onion, and herbs sizzling in oil. Once-cooked poke sprouts can also stand in for cucumbers as a sweet pickle. Or you can chop or blend once-cooked poke sprouts for a soup or soufflé.

Poke Soufflé mingles elegance with the taste of the wild. Begin with a cream or cheese sauce. Melt 2 tablespoons butter, stir in 2 tablespoons flour and a dash of salt. Mix in 1 cup milk or ¾ cup milk and ½ cup grated cheese. Prepare a cup of chopped or blenderized cooked poke sprouts. Separate 4 eggs. Beat their yolks and add them to the sauce. Stir in the poke. Now beat the egg whites until they stand stiff. Fold them into the green mixture and slide it into a straight-sided casserole. Bake it at 350 degrees F. (175 degrees C.) for about half an hour until it is brown and firm on top. Poke Soufflé makes a fine, light springtime meal when accompanied with a wild-weed salad. It will be a meal for the moment, because poke sprouts and other wild greens soon grow too tough and bitter to be eaten.

As pokeweed grows beyond the point where it is edible, its medicinal powers increase. Echoing Indian remedies all but forgotten, scientific literature refers more and more frequently to *Phytolacca americana,* suggesting that the poke plant may eventually yield remedies for modern ills including cancer. Scientists have isolated "phytomitogens" within the chemical composition of the plant. These substances stimulate cell growth and are being studied for antiviral and antibacterial properties. Poke's toxins effectively combat snail-carried schistosomiasis too, promising better health to millions of people in many parts of the world. The plant may be poisonous, but pokeweed seems willing to help humankind.

But poke should not be considered a home remedy. A minute, controlled dosage, knowledgeably prepared in a lab, may work wonders in the treatment of cancer and other ills. The household use of poke root could hurt, though. And children often reach for glistening poke berries, since they look as good as the blackberries the family picks together. But poke berries can also be lethal, and parents should not let children wander unobserved through the poke.

Some people won't pick poke because of these dangers; and at least one book marks it poisonous and warns never to eat it. My friend Sue Anne Elmore eats young poke sprouts raw. On the other hand, another friend, Margaret Sage, included in a salad just one raw leaf picked from a poke plant in full flower, and experienced diarrhea and vomiting for a day thereafter. But then I've also met a healthy fellow who eats cooked poke leaves on through the summer. He just cooks them longer as the year goes on, always in two or more waters. His

Phytolacca americana

practice may be risky, but it goes to show that poke can be benign if properly prepared.

Tradition passes down warnings about the poison in poke. I cook young sprouts in two waters, not because cooking full leaves once made me sick, but because most of those who have passed their knowledge on to me suggested the practice. Some vitamins are lost in the boiling, since both A and C are air- and water-soluble. But pokeweed fares high in both vitamins, providing 8,700 IUs of vitamin A and 136 milligrams of vitamin C, per 100 grams of greens, according to Euell Gibbons's figures. The deep green color of fresh, twice-cooked poke—cooked quickly, not boiled and boiled—reassures me. And my taste confirms my plan, since I find unpleasant the texture of both undercooked poke and poke greens that have grown too old. With so many spring sprouts and garden lettuce to munch raw, I enjoy the springtime pleasure of cooked poke salad. I've caught the gentle springing of a potent plant.

Essence of Spring

F L O R A L fragrance makes you swoon on a lusty day in May. Wild rose is out and honeysuckle's open. Thick aromas beckon you to lean down and take a deep, long breath. Let the sweet scent of spring fill your nose and mind as you drift along into the heat of summer. Autumn may be harvest time for fruits and nuts and vegetables. Spring is the time to harvest flowers.

The essence of spring flowers can be captured moist or dry, in a perfume or a potpourri. Any fragrant flower will add its share: honeysuckle, yucca bloom, wild or cultivated roses, even clover and mint flowers. Each flower must be preserved in its own special way, but all give up their essence if you follow a few simple rules.

The fragrance of flowers dwells in volatile oils, ingredients essential to the character of the plants that produce them. In some plants (like mints) the oil is so abundant that even the leaves give off a smell. In others, the oil concentrates in the flower and evaporates as the flower blooms. Floral scents attract passing insects, which find nectar in the plant's bursting sweetness. In passing, they distribute pollen from one bloom to the next and complete a cycle of floral insemination assuring that seeds will set.

There are two ways to capture the essence of spring. The first is to mingle the floral oils into an absorbent, neutral oil, creating a perfume.

Lonicera japonica

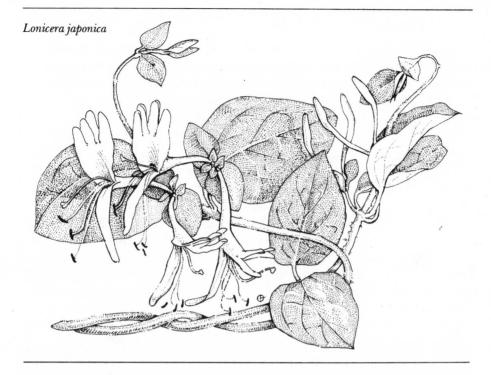

The second is to dry fragrant blossoms quickly, capturing the oil within them, to make a potpourri. Both processes take care and attention to the flowers' texture and to the weather.

For perfume, begin with an unscented oil. Safflower oil or pure mineral oil seems to work best. Pour three or four tablespoons of oil into a pint jar, then toss in four or five cotton balls. They should soak up the oil, so that none sloshes around in the bottom of the jar.

Start the process on the first day's blooming of whatever flower's essence you want to keep. Last spring I tried honeysuckle and wild rose. Next spring I'll try wild bergamot. In the early morning, after the dew is dry but before the sun sits overhead, fill your jar with fresh-opening flowers. Pack it gently, tightly close the lid, and let it sit all day in the sun. Continue this process daily, emptying yesterday's blooms, refilling the jar with today's fresh flowers, until the blossoming season ends. If it rains, bring the jar inside; avoid introducing water into the oils that you are gathering.

The hot sun draws the oil out from the flowers, just as it would had they stayed on the vine. As the day grows cooler the essential oils condense and mingle in the oil-soaked cotton. Each day you fill the jar with fresh flowers, and each day your neutral oil acquires a sweeter scent, borrowed from the flowers of spring. When blooming time is over, squeeze out the fragrant oils into a little vial. Keep it in the refrigerator for an occasional dash of springtime essence behind the ears. It may feel a little oilier than the perfumes you have known. It's not as pure as Chanel No. 5. But when you smell it you can almost see spring blooming, and you can smell it all winter long.

You cannot wear a potpourri, but you can keep it in your drawer or closet. A potpourri ("rotted pot" in French) consists of dried leaves and blossoms selected and preserved for color and fragrance. They mix and mingle over time, subtly ripening into a blend delightful for eyes and nose. Many potpourris use rose petals as a base because they are colorful, long-lasting, and fragrant. Some smell stronger than others; some dry with deeper reds. More than twenty varieties of roses grow wild across the continent, and of course many more bloom in flower gardens, homestead sites, and along frontyard picket fences. A potpourri made with several rose varieties, wild, found, or cultivated, has a good start.

Once again, pick your rose blooms in the early morning, but late enough so that the petals are dry. You can pick the buds or the entire blossoms, or you can pluck the petals from their center. They will dry more easily and you may return to find rose hips next winter (see "Rose Hips"). Toss the buds or petals into a shallow pan or stretched sheet of screen. Cover with cheesecloth to keep the wind from blowing them away. Set them in the sun, getting hotter day by day as it approaches the solstice.

Flowers dry adequately in the oven too. The warmer of a wood stove, a gas stove's pilot light, or the lowest temperature possible in an electric oven will dry flowers, preserving color and scent. Check them after half an hour of slow heat. If they still feel moist, check them every quarter hour thereafter.

On a good day, rose petals will dry outside in six hours. Buds will take several days. Bring them in as soon as they are dry. Check to be sure by placing them in a closed jar in the sunshine once again. If no condensation forms on the jar, you have dried them adequately. If condensation beads signal that the flowers are still moist, set them out in the sunshine tomorrow or on the windowsill if it rains.

I like to include in a potpourri other leaves and petals that remind me of spring. Honeysuckle and clover blossoms, while they shrivel down to nothing, still add fragrance from the fields. Mint leaves and evergreen fronds shade a potpourri green. Sassafras flakes add a forest twang. Experiment. When you find a flower whose fragrance you like, try drying it to include in your blend.

The dried petals should smell sweet and strong, but the fragrance will fade unless you fix it. Orrisroot is a natural fragrance fixative derived from a wild iris native to and now cultivated in Mediterranean countries. You can buy the chalky white root whole or powdered from many herb dealers and shops. Use the equivalent of one teaspoon of powdered fixative for each quart of potpourri. Sprinkle it into your pot, distribute it over the flowers. Keep your potpourri in a sealed container, and it will ripen over the year. Lift the lid for a whiff now and then. Spring floats back into view.

Miraculous Morels

SPRING has rained enough by now so that green enlivens the landscape. Sprigs of wild flora burst out everywhere, blotches of new color amidst the winter drab. Your eye seeks out every sign of new life. But, appealing as the greens may be, now is the time to notice, amidst the grays and browns of woods and orchard floors, the mushroom that some people around here in Virginia colloquially call a "merkle." I retrain my eyes each spring to find that gnomish brown fungus: the miraculous morel.

Morels are among the most positively identifiable mushrooms around. One almost always finds them growing at the base of old or dead trees. Abandoned apple orchards are the perfect place to look for them, scattered beneath each tree's declining limbs. When you see a merkle, you will know it: the stout hollow stem, light beige, almost iridescent. Atop the stem sits the darker confusion of spongy membranes, cone-shaped, ridged and pitted. Morels' only mushroom look-alikes are the false morels, some edible, some not. But false morel caps are not pitted; they are wadded close and tight. They appear less frequently than the true morels but sprout throughout the warm seasons. True morels poke up only after the first full spring rain, once warm weather sets in for good.

If you're leery about identifying morels, find someone who has gathered them before. Every area in which they thrive (throughout the temperate regions of the United States and Canada) has its resident group of mushroomers, old-timers and newcomers both, who know all about the morel. Ask them, and they'll tell you merkle stories all afternoon.

They'll tell you where to look—in this orchard or that burnt-out forest patch, under the tree stumps and around dead timber. They'll tell you when to look—when the peaches are blooming or as apple blossoms open up. They'll tell you the best weather for morels—when spring keeps the earth warm, when rain has soaked the ground and the warm air pulls those fungi right up out of the ground. Talk to folks who know, and they'll tell you to take a paper bag and a spoon or knife, and be ready for an afternoon of gathering. They'll warn you that morels come and go mysteriously, so if you see one you should pick it. Come back tomorrow and it will be gone.

And, if you find someone to tell you about morels, ask for some favorite recipes too. The classic preparation calls for trimmed mushrooms, sliced in half lengthwise. These are rinsed in salt water, drained and patted dry, then tossed in salted flour or cracker crumbs and fried till golden brown in real butter. Some mushroomers wouldn't think of doing anything else with morels, so as not to sully their delicate taste and texture.

But if you're lucky and find lots of morels, you'll discover other ways to use them too. Their curious shape can ornament many a dish. Slice them horizontally into wavy rings that peek out of a golden

Morchella esculenta

omelet or float in Cream of Morel Soup. Melt 4 tablespoons butter in a deep saucepan. Slice your morels—2 quarts if you've got them—and simmer them in the butter. Pull out the mushrooms, but use the juice to soften a thinly sliced onion, 3 thinly sliced celery stalks, and several cloves of wild garlic. Add a cup of vegetable broth and 3 cups of whole milk, including some cream if you want. Bring just to boiling; reduce heat and add the cooked mushrooms. Simmer without boiling, about 20 minutes. Season to your taste.

And if you're even luckier in finding morels and pick more than you can eat this spring, they freeze well. Rinse and drain them, then pack them in an airtight plastic bag for mushroom pleasures all year round. Merkles don't happen often—just a few warm, wet days in spring.

Wild Strawberries

W H E N settlers explored the tangled undergrowth of this New World, they were delighted by an abundance of wild strawberries. They recorded their discovery, naming the new variety after their queen and her new colony: they called the plant *Fragaria virginiana*. Europeans knew both wild and cultivated strawberries from their homelands, but the taste of these New World berries confirmed rumors of a newfound Eden.

Today explorers into orchards, fields, and sunny woodlands discover wild strawberries all over again. We taste the innocence of fruits grown by the earth alone, without human help or harm. We taste the paradise of early springtime sun and rain turned to nectar. Discovering wild strawberries in sunshiny fields some bright morning, we share a moment of revelation with the settlers of long ago.

The three-part strawberry leaf is evergreen and a little fuzzy. It stands straight up to meet the early spring elements and gathers for itself a tart green taste, good for herbal teas. A combination of strawberry, sorrel, and spearmint leaves brews into a zesty tea. Iced cold, it quenches thirst throughout the summer.

Strawberry leaves can be gathered any time you find them and used fresh or dried for tea. Hang clipped leaves upside down in a dry, dark place to preserve them. A tea of the leaves has for centuries been prescribed for digestive ailments, diarrhea, and dysentery. The leaves as well as the fruit provide vitamin C in plenty.

Wild strawberries aren't at all ostentatious like the strawberries you buy in the store. They are small, pebble-shaped, and deep scarlet. Often they nestle in under the protective canopy of their leaves. White blossoms peep out weeks before the berries appear. Mark the spot: come back a month later with time to spare.

Once the low-lying flowers have shed their petals, the bumpy center left behind collects moisture through roots and leaves, color from the sun, plumping up into a morsel of natural sweet. Wild

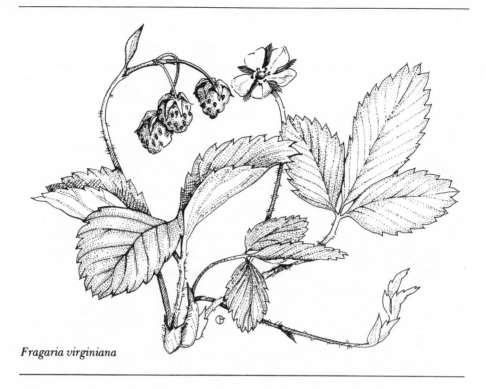

Fragaria virginiana

strawberries are miniature in comparison to cultivated, but they make up for small size with big flavor.

If you have major plans for wild strawberries—lots of jam or a strawberry pie—leave yourself plenty of picking time. Gather strawberries from midmorning on, as soon as the sun has dried off early-morning moisture. Take your time at it. You too will begin to absorb the moisture of the earth, the fire of the sky. Your fingertips will reflect the rich red of wild berries.

Consider gathering the berries in a container that won't drip or absorb their juices: a tin pail, plastic bucket, or wooden bowl will work better than a basket. And avoid having to handle those berries a second time by removing all leafy parts, stem and calyx, as you collect. The morning dew rinses them well; the sun dries them better than you could with a towel.

Be wary of the snakeberry as you gather. It masquerades as an edible fruit. Its leaves and berries seem to mimic the strawberry, but its fruit is distasteful, even dangerous in large quantities. It stays bright red all summer, long after the strawberries fade. Besides its bitter taste, the shape of the snakeberry distinguishes it. Bumpy rather than pockmarked, its seeds red instead of golden, snakeberries never flesh out the way strawberries do. Leave snakeberries for the animals, tempting as their color may be.

Some who find wild strawberries abundant in the wilds may want to transplant them closer to home. Prepare strawberry beds by spading the ground a foot deep and turning in a hearty compost. Collect single plants, scooping up a handful of dirt around each root system. Set the plants in two feet apart. Mulch the bed to keep in moisture and keep out weeds. Trim off the many runners that will shoot off your plants this summer, and snap off any flowers that form as well: send that growing energy back to the rootstock you have gathered. Next year, you can train a few runners into a constellation around the parent plant. It's possible to establish a wild strawberry bed in spring or in fall, but the plants will have to winter over before you can expect full fruiting.

Bring home a bowl of wild strawberries: everyone expects jellies and jams, shortcake and pie. But, besides tasting good, wild strawberries also have healing properties. Since the berries are astringent, they make a soothing facial mask. Crush half a cup of freshly gathered berries into a paste, adding a little water for the right consistency. Smooth the mixture on cheeks, chin, and forehead, sit back, and relax for a while. This strawberry mask is particularly helpful on sunburned skin. You might freeze small portions of strawberry pulp for later in the summer. When the sun beats down hard, bring out those springtime juices to cool the flame.

And of course save some wild strawberries for the simple pleasures. Toss a few on a bowl of breakfast cereal. Top a fruit compote with a scattering of red. The first to fruit, the favorite of many: wild strawberries herald a pungent summer.

SUMMER

Daylilies

T H E   S U N approaches its zenith. Hot rays coax daylilies abloom. Warm orange blossoms slowly explode for a single day of bliss, then fold forever. A summer day sees the daylily open, rejoice in the sunshine, share its pollen with the insects, sense the day's end, and close. The same abundance of activity fills a daylily's yearly cycle.

Even in the deep of winter, a cluster of nubby tubers multiplies underground. Small nut-shaped root parts, each with plant potential, spread from the growing center. The wild daylily never reproduces by seed. But to see the abundance of summer blossoms, one knows that the tubers have been active year round. Bright sprigs of foliage appear early, some of the first green to sprout in fields and streamsides. By late spring flower stalks have shot straight up, three or four feet high. Tender buds emerge, often twelve to a stalk; they blossom one by one, one a day. Spent blooms wither and fade and finally fall away. Stalks recede; tubers take over for another winter of underground hibernation.

At each stage of its yearly growth the daylily offers us food to forage. Through the winter, as long as the ground can be shoveled, daylily tubers come out tasting sweet and add wild crunch to your salads. They can be roasted too. Just be sure that each tuber feels firm to the touch; spongy tubers are dead and not too tasty. New shoots of daylily foliage, especially the blanched white inner leaves, will enhance a springtime salad too.

We can gather the daylily inflorescence, from promise to passing, for kitchen uses too. Green buds blushed with the orange to come

Hemerocallis fulva

belong in salads. They make interesting pickles too. Boil a syrup of 1 cup cider vinegar, ½ cup honey or 1 cup sugar, and ¼ cup pickling spices (see "Wild Spice" for pickling spices you can gather). Pour the boiling syrup over daylily buds packed in sterile jars. Seal and let them sit at least six months before tasting. How pleasant to nibble on daylily buds in midwinter, to see the flower curled up within.

But many won't want to clip daylilies in the bud. You can enjoy the blossoms and eat them too. Sometimes I pick a bouquet of these fine bright flowers to decorate our table, then gather dinner fare from the vase. Daylily Blossom Tempura makes a voluptuous summertime meal.

Whip up a batter just before cooking. Whisk the yolk of one egg with 2 cups ice-cold water. Sift in 1 cup white flour, ⅔ cup whole grain flour, ⅛ teaspoon soda, and ¼ teaspoon salt. Beat this batter briefly. It will seem quite runny but it will stick well to dry blossoms. Heat oil, preferably safflower or peanut, to medium-high heat in a wok or deep fat fryer. Batter-dip the blossoms, then fry to golden brown. You can plan an entire meal around this delicacy by preparing bite-size pieces of other vegetables and wild things. Try lamb's quarters sprigs, watercress leaflets, mint leaves, or elder blossoms, tofu, cheese squares, and fish chunks as well. Batter fry them all.

But some may even balk at clipping daylilies in the blossom. They could, like the Japanese, still gather the wilted flowers, drying them thoroughly to add to soups throughout the winter. Like okra in soup, daylily blossoms add substance and their own earthy flavor. To dry daylilies for storage, spread wilted blossoms on a newspaper or wax paper. Cover them with cheesecloth and keep them in a dark, breezy place until they crackle to the touch. The process will take about a week, depending on the weather. Or you could dry them in a very low oven overnight. In a tightly sealed jar, the dried flowers will keep deep into the winter, when daylily stalks have fallen and daylily spirit has sunk underground.

Yarrow

IN THE EARLY spring, deep green feathery clumps of yarrow appeared. Crushed, the leaves shared a sweet, biting, herby odor. Now, in summer, flowers borrow the smell. With the hot weather, yarrow stretches into a tall, slender stalk. Its feathery foliage comes to smell more vegetative. White flowers exhale bitter sweetness into the air. Something about its fragrance sets me spinning. When I breathe deeply of the yarrow blossom, my imagination wanders back into fragrant, dusty afternoons alone in my grandmother's attic. I take in must and mothballs, old lace and old photographs. Yarrow smells like forgotten memories.

Yarrow's roots reach deep into history and myth. Homer tells us that the centaur Chiron, who conveyed herbal secrets to his human pupils, taught Achilles to use yarrow as a "woundwort" on the battlegrounds of Troy. History tells us that knights treated wounds with the same herb in the British Isles and, apparently, so did several Indian tribes in North America. No one is sure whether yarrow grew here wild before the Europeans settled or whether colonists brought the plant with them. If they brought it, setting it free in their campsites and gardens, yarrow must have taken off and traveled westward faster than the pioneer movement. Because, when adventurers made their way across the continent, they found Indians treating wounds with yarrow.

Yarrow grows native in the Orient too, revered in myth and valued in practice. Oriental tradition assured mountain wanderers that where the yarrow grew neither tigers nor wolves nor poisonous plants would be found. So beneficent was the yarrow in Oriental culture that sages used its stalks to consult the *I Ching,* the ancient Chinese book of fortune. Fifty fifteen-inch-long stalks, stripped of leaves and flowers, were divided, counted, and set out in a pattern over and over again. Like leaves in a tea cup the stalks answered any questions posed. Psychologist C. G. Jung believed that spiritual agencies "acting in a mysterious way . . . make the yarrow stalks give a meaningful answer." With the stalks, one reaches toward truth in the *Book of Changes* almost as one might seek the divine.

Western European tradition, curiously schizoid, connects yarrow with a goddess and a demon both. Yarrow is a witching herb, used to summon the devil or drive him away. But it is also a loving herb in the domain of Aphrodite. Nursery rhymes jingle that if you put a yarrow sachet under your pillow, you will dream of your own true love. Or perhaps you'll see your love and the devil walking side by side.

Yarrow's reputation for spirit may originate in its healing powers. Taken internally in a cup of tea, yarrow relieves cramps, expels gas, and reduces swelling. It also sweats out a fever, as some folks put it. Take a cup of yarrow tea when you feel a cold coming. You'll sleep

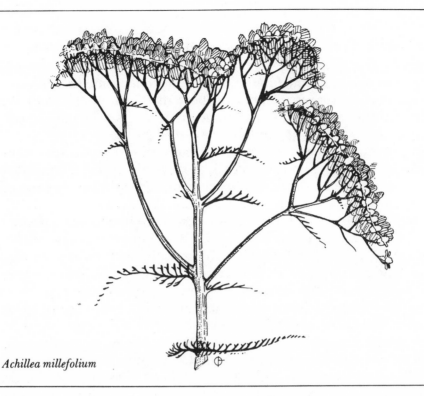

Achillea millefolium

hard and sweat profusely and may awaken with the cold behind you. Yarrow tea is a tonic as well, strengthening the inward body if the tea is drunk regularly. Chinese proverbs claim that yarrow brightens the eyes and promotes intelligence. Worldwide culture offers reasons, fact or fantasy, to add a sprig of yarrow to every summer pot of herbal tea.

Abundant throughout most of the United States and Canada, yarrow is easy to find and a pleasure to gather. It flowers early in the summer, along with the daisies and daylilies here in Virginia. One dry summer morning of each year, I go out to gather an armful of yarrow stalks, pungent leaves and flowers opening their bloom. I hang them in small bundles, flowertops down, in a dark, breezy place. An attic would do well. If I'm lucky, the next week's weather will stay dry and I can pull down well-cured yarrow.

I cut off the flowerheads and put them in one jar for sachets, potpourris, and tea. I strip off the leaves and put them in another jar to use for healing. Each year I renew my bundle of fifty yarrow stalks which I use to consult the *I Ching*. I continue to let some yarrow grow in my garden, too. Some herbals report that yarrow enhances the flavor of herbs growing near it. Some gardeners say its odor repels invading insects (see "Wild Herbs in the Garden").

Yarrow smells green and acrid, like many other herbs traditionally grown for cooking. The fragrance is so strong you understand that yarrow is a seasoning herb to be used in moderation like oregano or thyme, not a potherb to be eaten like lamb's quarters or amaranth greens. On a wild spring salad, I enjoy a creamy white dressing flecked with the green of the yarrow herb. Blend together any of the following: sour milk, buttermilk, sour cream, mayonnaise, cottage cheese. Add about one-fifth that volume in vinegar. Season as you like: salt, black pepper, dry mustard, cayenne. Sprinkle dried or fresh yarrow green into the dressing. Three or four fronds, chopped or shattered, flavor a cup and a half of dressing nicely.

The scent of yarrow opens up the nostrils. The thought of yarrow opens the imagination too, inviting me to add my own stories to the traditions that emanate from this common weed. I use the yarrow and I let it grow in yard and garden. Its fragrance evokes ancient days and fortunes yet to come. Yarrow invites interpretation.

Lamb's Quarters

L A M B ' S quarters is one of those wild plants whose virtues have been lost in tradition. Somewhere along the way it picked up the common name pigweed—a term I try to avoid, since people use it for several unrelated weeds. Apparently lamb's quarters gained a

Chenopodium album

reputation some time back as a plant fit for fodder: for hogs but not for humans. The word "pigweed" came into use in the mid-1800s, as the railroads cut through to the West. It seems that white settlers used the term for many plants that nourished the tribes they were displacing. The plants survived the attack, but continue to suffer a misnomer. Let's bring all the plants called pigweed—lamb's quarters, purslane, wild amaranth, probably some others—back into the human fold.

The nutritional facts on these so-called pigweeds are compelling. Lamb's quarters is a good example. An adult needs about 5,000 international units of vitamin A daily. A half cup of lamb's quarters offers 14,000 to 16,000 IUs, depending on the season. We need about

70 milligrams of vitamin C each day. Lamb's quarters, again half a cup, gives 66 to 130 milligrams of vitamin C. Over the summer, the vitamin A content of lamb's quarters increases while the vitamin C content goes down. Lamb's quarters offers significant plant protein, supplies over one-third the adult daily requirement for calcium (about 309 milligrams in half a cup), and provides one of the highest fiber contents of any vegetable, wild or cultivated. And it tastes good too.

Lamb's quarters grows profusely throughout the continent of North America, in city lots and country fields alike, preferring scrubby spaces, compost piles, and garden corners to the wide-open places. Once you know its shield-shaped leaf, passing through variations with the seasons, you will see it everywhere.

Lamb's quarters grows to three, four, even five feet tall when we let it. Secondary stalks branch out from a thick ribbed spine. The leaves are jagged diamonds, dark green with a frosty sheen that intensifies in toward each budding center. As summer proceeds, lamb's quarters' leaves dwindle and seeds develop. The leaves respond visibly to difficult conditions, mottling red and yellow and blue when the air gets too cold or the soil too spent. But under most conditions lamb's quarters grows full and healthy all summer long. Its leaves have substance, like spinach or kale, their color the bluest of the weedy greens.

Lamb's quarters can get woody as summer moves on. A good rule of thumb is, if you can break it off easily you can chew it easily too. Gather just the tender tips as the plant grows large. The bunching green flowers concentrate its high food value. So do the star-shaped seeds, which can be harvested for winter cooking. Chop down a whole plant once the seeds have formed. Hang it upside down in a cool dry place. Spread newspapers under it to catch falling seeds or enclose each plant in a paper bag. When the plant is dry enough so that a leaf will crackle, shake the seeds onto papers or into a bag. Some chaff will remain. You can separate it in the wind, before a fan or hair blower, or in small quantities just by gently puffing. Or you can tolerate the chaff—it's just dried lamb's quarters. Sprinkle gathered seeds over omelets or casseroles for a protein-rich garnish.

I use lamb's quarters all summer long to add green to a meal, whether cooked or in a salad. I stir-fry onions, garlic, and lamb's quarters into an omelet for breakfast, a meal that reminds me of a morning several years ago, when my friend Erbin stirred green leaves into our eggs and I wondered, weeds for breakfast? Now I eat lamb's quarters many a morning: how my life has changed. I also add lamb's quarters sprigs to many summer salads.

Lamb's quarters can even grace an elegant dish like a quiche. Margaret Haupt said I could share her recipe. Begin with a nine-inch pie shell. (For a ten-inch shell, double the recipe.) Beat together 2 eggs, 1 cup cream, a minced onion or a quarter cup wild garlic cloves, a dash of salt, and a dash of cayenne pepper. Layer into the shell ½ cup shredded Swiss or mozzarella cheese, 1 cup chopped lamb's quarters, and the beaten egg mix. Sprinkle the pie with wood sorrel, parsley, or more chopped lamb's quarters. Bake at 425 degrees F. (218 degrees C.) for 15 minutes, then reduce heat to 300 degrees F. (150 degrees C.) and bake half an hour more. Let the quiche stand five minutes before cutting into it. What a treat!

Neither the taste, the texture, nor the nutritional riches of lamb's quarters warrant the condescension registered in its common name "pigweed." Some people still pull up these weeds and feed them to the pigs. They raise healthy animals, to be sure. But others, with human friends and family to feed, are beginning to discover what pigs have known for quite a while. Lamb's quarters is a valuable weed.

Wild Herbs in the Garden

GARDEN vegetables must seem irresistible to insects. After roaming the fields, where acrid herbs season the air, insects zero in on a sweet garden plot. Down those scavengers swoop, benefiting from your hours of loving cultivation. But you can bring repellent herbs into your garden from the wild. You can disguise your garden as just another field in the hope that pests will pass it by.

Mints have the reputation for being insect repellents. Bring in a few plants from stream or field, and they will discourage insect visitations as they mature into harvestable herbs for tea. Usually the scent makes mint identification easy, but these plants share other characteristics. A square stem and opposing leaves always mark a mint. Once you have seeded your garden, you can transplant wild seedlings of pennyroyal, catnip, or other mints into your garden to tuck into empty spaces. Their fragrance will cheer you, even as it keeps marauders out.

Pennyroyal has the smallest leaves and the tartest odor of the native mints. Nurseries often sell European varieties of the plant as an herbal groundcover. But taller stands of American pennyroyal grow wild here, coast to coast. I've seen it filling fields in northern California and timbered clearings in the Virginia mountains where I live. Small opposing leaves cling to straight-standing stalks, up to eight inches tall. Tiny blue flowers twinkle where leaves and stalks meet. Pennyroyal is so fragrant that even its winter remains, the skeletal stalk and flower, give off a strong whiff of mint. Dried bunches of pennyroyal that Erbin and I gathered a year and a half ago still smell when I brush past them. Pennyroyal really smells as if it would repel insects, with its fierce, volatile scent.

Native Americans used pennyroyal for many ills, and Anglo medicine accepted it as a useful herb. It has been sipped and sniffed for colds, headaches, sore eyes, and difficult menstrual periods. In fact, pennyroyal tea was used as an abortive by American natives and settlers. In light of that tradition (even though, to the best of my knowledge, medical science has not yet confirmed the report), happily pregnant women should avoid consuming pennyroyal. I try to drink pennyroyal tea instead of popping aspirin on days when my period gets me down. I brew a pot of what I euphemistically call my "minstrel tea," adding to pennyroyal fresh or dried leaves of other mints, strawberry, yarrow, and periwinkle. It tastes and feels good.

Catnip is another soothing mint that can do double duty as a garden repellent. Organic gardeners claim that catnip directly affects the flea-beetle population—those tiny, hopping black specks that go

Satureja calamintha

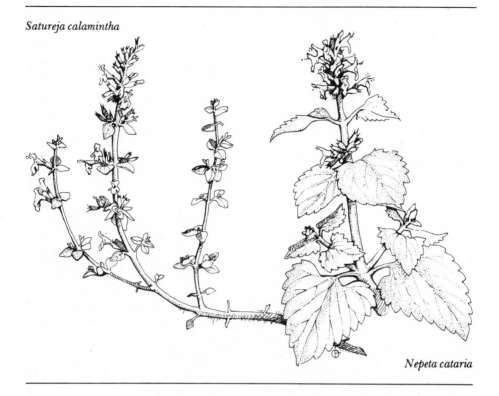

Nepeta cataria

for eggplants first. When I set in a row of eggplants last summer, I noticed a flea beetle invasion within days. I brought into that neighborhood a few seedlings of catnip, sprouting off a large plant I had transported from the wild. All eggplants revived, freed of flea beetles, and I grew great bouquets of catnip as well.

It may have been brought here by colonists, but catnip ranges free these days. I've found it standing in open spaces along the Appalachian Trail and in the downtown alleys of Ann Arbor, Michigan. It smells different wherever I find it, but always has that sweet, soporific smell, a little like other mints, but stuffier. It always has fuzzy white heart-shaped, scallop-edged leaves and terminal clusters of light lavender blooms. It lasts into cold weather and, unlike our native pennyroyal, it grows perennially.

Settlers must have brought catnip with them for its calming powers.

European tradition designates catnip the tea to drink for shattered nerves, splitting headaches, and overexcited children. It soothes the stomach and the soul. Nowadays we associate catnip with cats alone, but humans have found pleasure in this herb as well. Some claim that smoking catnip can produce a legal high. It makes a contribution, at least, to the flavor of a good herbal smoke (see "Summer Smoke").

Either of these mints will help your garden. So will many others, tossed into fields by winds that carry seed or planted long ago at some homestead doorstep. Mints thrive in the wild, but I think they would rather be adopted. From some, like catnip, you can gather autumn seed. But at this time of the year, particularly before they flower, all mints can be safely transplanted, secure in a clod of dirt, into the garden. Yarrow can be brought into the garden now too. Not only does it wave away marauding insects; it also sweetens the soil for herbs and vegetables around it.

Bit by bit, I weave into my garden fragrant weeds from the wild. Catnip bushes up near blooming tomatoes, pennyroyal stands near the peas. Squash vines entwine a bending stand of yarrow. As the vegetables bulge ripe, the herbs bloom hardy. I bring both in with the harvest for health and warmth through the long winter's night.

Cattails

No ONE has trouble recognizing cattails. That long, tall shape, which we've seen in landscape paintings and autumnal bouquets since childhood, is so familiar. We hardly notice stands of cattails lining our highways. Cattails just belong there. Each year they undertake a primitive yet intricate cycle of growth and flowering

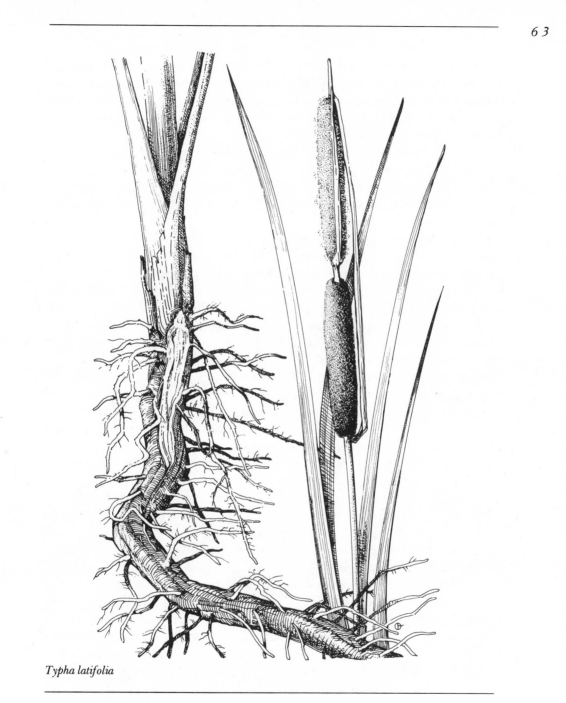

Typha latifolia

that culminates in the conventional image of a brown velvet cob. But native dwellers of six continents—North Americans three hundred years ago and Australian aborigines today—have noticed in detail the cycles of the cattail, for they have found abundant uses for many of its growing parts.

As each new part of the cattail plant emerges, green and tender, it is edible. Root buds in winter, young green shoots in spring, green flowers in spring and early summer. Even the bright yellow pollen as it seeks to leave its source can be collected at just the right moment and used or stored for later, a bright yellow addition to any grainy dish. You can consider that the cattails, most common among them *Typha latifolia,* are safe for the trying. Not all may be palatable at every phase of growth, but many are good and none will harm you.

Cattail shoots have received the most acclaim as "Cossack asparagus," named for peasant soldiers from the Ukraine who foraged for the blanched inner shoots of spring cattails, rarely finding them as tasty as those that grew along the banks of their home river, the Don. But cattail roots and cattail pollen deserve their share of the praise, delicious and nutritious as they both are.

Cattail roots and cattail pollen, the origin and the outpouring of this useful plant, call for entirely different methods of gathering and use. Cattail roots can be gathered all winter long, while for cattail pollen one must catch the moment in late spring or early summer when bright gold dust begins to scatter. Cattail roots require long and intricate preparation, but one uses cattail pollen as is.

Cattail roots branch, creep, and thread their way down into the mud of marshes, swamps, and streams. They will achieve a diameter of up to two inches, and with their firm, white flesh they invite experimentation. Geese and muskrats seek them out, so Bradford Angier says. Native Americans found them to be a source for a sweet, substantial gruel. The easiest way to obtain cattail root starch, which improves the taste and texture of any baked bread, is to filter the starch through water. Gather about five six- to eight-inch lengths of cattail root for each cup of flour in a favorite bread recipe. Prepare the roots as follows.

Scrub the dirt off the outside of the roots. Into a clean pot or bowl filled with water, break or slice open each root lengthwise. You can feel coagulant clusters of starch and the long fibers running lengthwise through the root. Work with the roots, trying to dislodge and dissolve the starch into the water. The fibers will stay strung to the root skin. Put the bowl of starchy water aside, and in half an hour the starch will settle. Pour off the water, add more, and work with the roots once again. You can feel the starchy results of your labor. Go at it as long as you sense more starch yet to dissolve.

The remaining thick white paste, something like cornstarch mixed with water, I add to cornbread, biscuits, waffles. You can add it to your favorite baking recipe too. Or try my favorite cattail biscuits. The recipe calls for a total of 3 cups of meal, flour plus cattail starch. I like to use about a cup of cattail starch and 2 cups of whole grain flour, but you can try whatever you have on hand.

Cut ¾ cup butter into your flour, mixed with 4½ teaspoons baking powder and ¾ teaspoon salt. Beat 3 eggs, then beat into them your portion of cattail starch and ½ cup of milk. Combine the wet ingredients with the mealy flour; toss them lightly together with a wooden spoon. Add up to ¼ cup more milk if you need it for proper texture. Knead the biscuit dough; roll and fold it for flakiness. Roll it out one-half inch thick. Cut into 2-inch circles. Bake in a hot oven (450 degrees F., 230 degrees C.) for 10 to 15 minutes. You will taste the difference between these biscuits and the same recipe made without the cattail starch. You will feel the difference too. The cattail starch lends a smooth, glutinous consistency to these high-rising biscuits.

Winter is the best time to gather cattail roots, either for the starch or for the tasty buds of next year's stalks, edible raw or cooked. But late spring or early summer is the best time to keep watch for cattail pollen, produced by the male half of the spiky cattail flower. This season, take a look at the cattail inflorescence or flowering process. So often we envision the cattail as a static image, a cigar on a stick. But those flowering parts grow and change through spring and summer. First a papery sheath encloses two distinct parts, the male spike above and the green female cob, potential seedbed, beneath. Sunshine stimulates a bursting out from the male flower: bright yellow pollen parts at a touch. Those particles that escape your reach will settle on waiting female flowers, the lower half of the process, triggering reformation into a tightly packed cluster of winged seeds—that cylindrical formation we commonly envision as a cattail.

You won't stop the process if you draw off a little pollen. Plenty will escape you. Carry a quart jar into which you can bend and tap the shedding stalks. If you gather pollen from about twenty-five cattail flowerheads, you should be able to follow the very same biscuit recipe above, substituting one cup of cattail pollen for one cup of cattail root starch. Of course requirements for liquid will vary, and you need to stir the pollen in with the flour before starting. The recipe will bake up into admirable biscuits, tinted golden with sunny summer pollen, yet sharing some sweet, subtle flavor with their winter counterparts. Or substitute cattail pollen for some part of the flour in any other recipe for baking.

As you learn to use cattails, remember the millions of others on all six continents who have gathered this benign and generous plant—not only for food, but also to make building foundations, shoes, spears, walls, partitions, ropes, mats, sieves and baskets, quilts, cushions, diapers, shrouds, sleeping bags, life preservers, sound and heat insulation. Native healers found cattail flowers an external remedy for burns, wounds, and ulcers; found a tea of the leaves helpful against uterine or rectal hemorrhaging; and found the roots useful for women and animals in labor, to promote contractions and expel the placenta. A folk cure for diarrhea uses cattail rootstock, boiled in milk. It is sweet, bland, and nutritious, and even a skeptical partner or squeamish child might try this healthful herbal cure.

For thousands of years, human tribes have noticed cattails growing in wet places, found them friendly, and put them to use. Despite our modern-day obliviousness of their presence, cattails still thrive among us. In the last thirty years, a few voices have cried out for reconsideration of the cattail's plentiful yield. Syracuse University actually instituted a Cattail Research Center, to further knowledge and promote cultivation of the wild cattail. I add my voice to those few others, urging not to plough and cultivate so much as simply to notice and enjoy the ever-present cattail.

Clovers

TAKING a walk with a goat can bring inspiration to anyone who likes to gather wild things. A goat nuzzles into the foliage, seeking ripe leaves and tender twiglets to munch on. She steps out into the green world, which can offer her full fare, fresh and free, the year round. In winter she crunches into honeysuckle, greenbrier, and the tops of ice-felled trees. In spring she nibbles growing sprigs of poison ivy and the bulging buds of sassafras and dogwood. Autumn ripens poke berries; down fall leaves of sycamore and tulip poplar to her. Summer brings her clover.

Red clover borders fields and forests wherever it can, stretching over neighbor plants to a lazy height of a foot. It grows plump flowerheads, more a lavender or fuchsia than the red its name suggests. Red clover flowers make a mouthful for a goat, sweet and fibrous. I follow suit, chewing on a few slender flower parts pulled from the central stalk. Good enough to sprinkle on a salad for color. Sweet enough to add to a potpourri.

I also gather whole clover flowers, with neighbor leaves attached, to brew an herbal tea. Red clover tea, made from fresh or dried flowers, brews thick and golden in color. It tastes sweet and soothes a ticklish throat or situation. A cup of red clover tea helps me regain the silent, steady composure of a goat. I often toss a few easy-to-find red clover flowers into a mixed summer brew—herb tea made hot, then iced for summertime refreshment.

At the peak of clover's blooming, usually early in the summer, I go out with clippers in hand and gather up the plumpest, ripest clover flowers, including about four to six inches of stem and leaves with them. I hang them upside down in a dark, breezy place until they dry—two weeks if the weather is right—then I bottle up my clover herb for tea all winter long. Clover tea is an especially good cold treatment: it works directly on a throat that wants to cough. That

Trifolium pratense

warm, grassy smell evokes memories of the sunshiny day when clover
bloomed. Images of sunshine in the mind can hasten a wintry cold
away.

Farmers have sown the seed of clover for centuries. Indeed they
probably brought red clover to this continent on purpose, although
native clovers grew wild here already. Like other leguminous plants,
clover hosts root-dwelling bacteria that collect nitrogen from the air
and release it for use in the earth. Dig up a healthy clover plant, roots
and all. You'll see white nodules clustering among the root hairs, signs
of the symbiotic balance between nitrogen-fixing bacteria and their
hosts, the clover roots. By alternating clover with plants which deplete

the soil's nitrogen, like corn, rye, wheat, or sorghum, farmers help the soil strike a healthy balance.

Not only does clover provide green growing fertilizer. It also offers ideal fodder for cows and horses as well as for goats. Sweet and tasty and highly nutritious, clover will provide a large proportion of the plant protein needed by those husky animals. It can't help but nourish us too.

Nature probably sowed most of the clover you'll see this summer. It can take over in patches of the garden or the lawn. Let it! It will do you and your soil much good. Every variety of clover is safe and sweet, even if not all clovers taste as good to the human palate as they do to the goat's. But, just for the sake of a moment's imagining, take a bite of the next clover you see. Remember the goats, and remember me.

Elder Blow, Elderberries

IN EUROPE a spirit inhabits the elder bush. A dryad perches in its branches, turning elder blow to berries. She communicates with spirits dwelling elsewhere. Some say she even wards off the devil, and they borrow elder boughs to drape their doorways for protection.

Our North American elderberries are a slightly different species, but I'll bet a spirit haunts them too. Dark and tawny and somewhat more primitive (as I envision her), the native American spirit of *Sambucus* oversees the elderberry season from budding to fruition. She touches the tiny parchment flowers with subtle fragrance. She graces the berries with blue-black luster. She's tricky, too, raising high her berry clusters and setting down her roots in gullies just beyond human reach. But the elderberry spirit makes up for inaccessibility with cross-country abundance. Come the start of summer, wide white bouquets bloom throughout the continent. Come summer's end, dense clusters of purple berries droop extravagantly. The cycle of summer sees the elder blossom, fruit, and fade.

The elder flowers, called "blow" for their frothy white looks, can be gathered for food or medicine. If you don't mind sacrificing the berries-to-be, whole flowerheads can be clipped, dipped in a sweet batter, and fried as Elder Blow Fritters. Use the tempura recipe suggested for daylilies or the simple batter suggested for dandelion blooms.

To store the blooms for tea, hang them upside down in a dark, dry place, inside a paper bag or pillowcase. Soon they'll shed their ivory petals. Save them to brew a sweet tea to treat head colds or the blahs. You can brew a tea of leaves and flowers for a gentle antiseptic wash, to be used outside the body only. Do not drink a tea made from elder leaves; only bloom and berries are safe for eating.

To eat the elder blossoms, you can also coax them off the stem, leaving behind the fruit to form. Gather between a half and a full cup of elder petals to try the old favorite, Elder Blow Pancakes. Combine 2 cups of flour, 3 teaspoons baking powder, 1 teaspoon salt with 3 egg yolks, beaten together with 1 cup milk, 1 cup water, ½ cup oil, and 1 tablespoon honey. Stir all ingredients until they are just blended. Beat the 3 egg whites until stiff. Fold them into the batter along with your elder flowers. Spoon onto a hot greased griddle. The flowers melt right into the batter and make these hotcakes golden and fluffy.

Alongside early elder blossoms, unopened buds may still remain. In their lovely *Wild Food Recipe Book* (available from The Farmers' Way, P.O. Box 601, Taylors, South Carolina), Michael and Kay Farmer offer this recipe for Elder Bud Relish: wild green on the side. Make a syrup of ½ cup sugar, 1 cup water, and 2 cups cider vinegar. Bring the syrup to a boil. Add 3 cups elder buds removed from their stems, 1 finely chopped onion, 1 clove garlic (or more if you use wild garlic cloves), and 1 teaspoon salt. Make a spice bag out of cheesecloth to hold 1 sliced lemon and 1 tablespoon pickling spices (see "Wild Spice"). Boil everything together until the relish thickens, then pour it into sterile jars and seal.

Sambucus canadensis

The elder flowers you leave behind ripen into taut blue-black pellets, hung in a pendent network, a flat head of fruit. They glisten in the sun of a steamy August morning. They bulge. They drop. A handful popped into the mouth may be a disappointment, until you recall that within that tart fruit taste lie nutrients—vitamins A and C, iron, calcium, potassium—in abundance. Too bad we can't eat an apple's worth of elderberries a day. But thank goodness our jams come fortified.

There are probably as many elderberry jams as there are elderberry jam makers. Many just make it straight, adding ½ cup of water to each quart of berries, boiling them until they burst, then adding a cup or two of sweetening and slowly cooking the fruit to jam that spreads. I spice mine up with a sprig of wild ginger or a sprinkling of sassafras root bark. Others toss in early apple slices or ripe crabapples to lighten the flavor and add more natural pectin. Elderberry jam is hard to fail at, and even unjelled jam pours well over waffles.

How strange that a plant which feeds us so abundantly well could also harm us—but elderberry bushes can. Although a leaf tea will help the complexion, it would be poisonous to drink. All growing parts of the plant, except the flowering, fruiting portion, could be harmful. Only buds, flowers, and fruit can be eaten. Only the spirit sitting in the elderberry bush knows why.

Rubus Berries

SUMMER is for picking berries. I go out early, to find summer-morning steam surrounding the berries that I gather. I pluck one, and it fills my mouth with sweet, rich liquid that tastes like the heat of summer. A hint of green fruit lingers but the berry sings sweet. Summer berries dangle here and there across at least three other continents, but they cover our own. I'll bet that ninety percent of the berries I have seen in my lifetime remained unplucked. Or, pecked by passing birds, they traveled elsewhere, maybe to start a new patch of briers.

One variety after another comes ripe as summer passes by. Six weeks ago the pastures and hillsides were snowflaked with blossoms of raspberry, blackberry, dewberry. Now these plants are coming to fruition. Black raspberries are brimful of sweet juices. Dewberries are ready too. Blackberries are still green but getting redder by the day. Soon you won't have to look far through fields and woodland clearings to find berries to bring home by the basketful.

All these berries belong to the genus *Rubus,* named from the Latin word for red. All of them pass through red on the way to ripeness, although many turn a red so deep it's black. Rubus berries develop as a cluster of juicy beads, each containing a seed within. Except for the dewberry, all stand as single-stalk shrubs, bending down with the weight of berries. All their stems have stickers—of varying ferocity— and their flimsy, jagged leaves usually grow in clusters of three or five.

Black raspberries ripen first. Their stalks clinch the identification. Those that hold berries are purple-red with a white waxy finish. First-year canes stay pale aqua green. Scouting for berries, you may see this tall, pale growth from afar. New stalks shoot six feet high, signaling more mature neighbors bending over with berries nearby. You will know from the first bite whether black raspberries are ripe. But to avoid a bitter mouthful, take only those dark-blue berries that the plant gives up willingly. Any berry you must tug won't be worth the picking.

The red raspberry is next in line for ripening. The summer sun opens its furry fruit buds and fat green berries gain red. The wild red raspberry comes closest to the cultivated kind: velvet smooth, juicy, and tender. Its stalks often reveal a downy layer of harmless thorns. At about the same midsummer moment dewberries ripen. These trailing blackberries sport springtime blossoms like those of their elevated cousins, but they hold them close to the ground. Then summer warmth turns blossoms into fat black fruits. A dewberry stalk will trail a yard or more underfoot over cleared ground in fields and forests, bearing grand berries with large, jewel-like drupelets.

The more common blackberry bramble grows everywhere: in town and in the country, in mountain forests and lowland pastures, along the road and hidden away in lonely places. Blackberry stands show up in the spring, when their fleecy white blossoms call everyone's attention. The bright red fruits, unripe but bulging with promise, draw notice too. Let that red go black before you pick them, and remember to wear full-body clothing that won't snag when you go berry picking. You may have to fight through briers to get them, but these juicy berries are worth a scratch or two.

You may discover nearby raspberry or blackberry patches that you would like to cultivate. Pruned, weeded, and mulched, rubus canes will offer better fruit year by year. Each cane goes through a two-year cycle of life. The first year, a shoot sprouts up, like those six-foot aqua stalks from the black raspberry. The second year, branches emerge from the

Rubus spp.

single shoot; at their tips appear flowers, then fruit. Third-year canes die, but right beneath them perennial roots are shooting up new growth. In the case of the black raspberry, the tip of a stalk often grounds itself, establishing roots in the third year for a new plant.

Pruning works best in late summer, after fruiting, or in the early spring before new growth starts. Clear out other plants, dead briers, and the stalks that produced last season's fruit. Thin out the remaining stalks to allow comfortable picking, leaving plants spaced three to five feet apart. Then prune your remaining rubus briers back to the trimmest fruit-producing form—short stalks with several secondary branches, also cut short. Cut central canes off at a height of about three feet. Clip their offshoots, leaving only two to five buds per branch. From the few budding sprigs that you leave will spring next year's fruit. You'll transform a confused and drooping bramble into a trim, efficient berry bush. A thick mulch of hay or lawn clippings will keep the berry patch weedless and moist.

Doubtless you already have your favorite ways of using the rubus berries. I need hardly offer more. Instead I will share one of my lesser triumphs. Two summers ago I gathered three quarts of big, juicy dewberries. I crushed them and added a quart of water. I then set the mixture aside to ferment into wine, but made the mistake of covering the crock with a towel rather than an airtight lid. A month later, the rich but sour brew smelled more than anything like sweet vinegar. Still, I strained the liquid and bottled it. Six months later, while planning a party in celebration of the first Calendar of Wild Things, it occurred to me that my friends would like a taste of dewberry wine. I went to sample it, but, when I cracked the lid, I noticed a champagne-like fizz rising. So I kept the bottle shut until the party.

Only that evening, when I twisted off the lid, did I realize the problems inherent in bottling fizzy wine with a screw-on top. A well-dressed fellow whom I did not even know went home with deep red dewberry fizz all over his corduroy blazer. My friend Tom Cogill went home and dyed the rest of his shirt purple. His boots still show the stains. The dewberry disaster tasted like exceptionally sweet, thick, purple vinegar. I mixed in other beverages and served it anyway.

I have since learned how to make a tamer rubus berry wine, thanks to Bertha Ross. Here's her technique. Squeeze fully ripe berries to get the juice flowing. Add to the berries an equal amount of water. Place them in a crock, cover it with a tight-fitting lid, and let it sit a week, stirring daily. Strain the liquid through cheesecloth to sift out the seeds. Squeeze each handful of berries as you strain them to get all the juice you can. Add about one pound of sugar per gallon of berry juice. Taste it now for sweetness and add more sugar as needed. It should be tart but pleasing to the taste. Store it in screw-top bottles but (as I learned too well) leave the tops loose until the fermentation stops. That should take three to six weeks. Lean your ear to the bottle, and you'll hear the bubbles. Seal the bottles only when you hear bubbles no more. Let the bottled wine sit at least a couple of months. It improves with age.

Probably you and family and friends could easily devour all the rubus berries you gather, eating them for breakfast, lunch, and dinner under the hot solstice sun. But remember what joys these berries will bring when the sun is in winter shadow. One can preserve them simply by packing sterile jars full of berries, filling with boiling syrup (1 cup sugar or ½ cup honey to 2 cups water), sealing, then submerging sealed jars in a boiling water bath for fifteen minutes. A jar of ruby black berries from the cupboard warms my winter spirit from within with memories of spring blossoms and summer fruiting, their sweetness and their thorns.

Wild and Clean

SCRAMBLING through the woods, ploughing through the fields, bringing home armloads of roots and weeds: gathering wild things can be a dirty business. Some of you may even shrink from going out and gathering for fear of what it will do to your clothing, your hands, your floors. This chapter is for you. It's true that

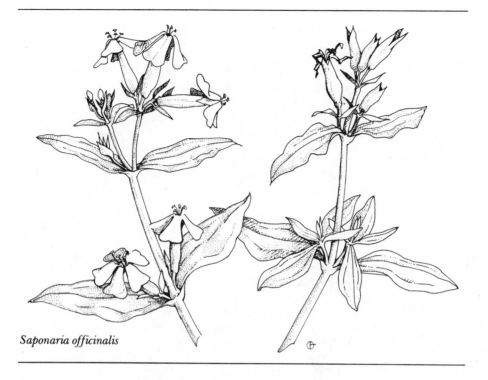

Saponaria officinalis

gathering wild things may make you dirtier. But you can gather wild things to make you come clean as well.

In fact, colonists brought soapwort (or bouncing bet, as it's affectionately called) to grow in their gardens as a soap source. Its Latin name, *Saponaria officinalis,* reflects recognition of it by seventeenth- and eighteenth-century botanists as the official soap plant. Active ingredients called "saponins" foam up and dislodge dirt particles. I use soapwort in the fields or in the garden, a ready source of soap for dirty hands. But others use it to cleanse fine fabrics, glass, and china. It seems not only to clean but also to fortify aging silks, brocades, and wools.

Bouncing bet pops into the landscape in early summer and stays all season. Bouquets of pink splash the countryside. The easiest way to discover soapwort's soap is to pick a handful of leaves and flowers. Wet them and rub them between your hands. A fresh, grassy scent and cool green lather will arise. Try it on dirty hands and face—it cleans.

To store soapwort for use during the cooler months when blossoms

Yucca filamentosa

are not around, gather its shallow, woody roots. Scrub the roots and dry them in two-inch lengths. Whenever you want a gentle natural detergent, put a few soapwort root chunks into a pot of water and simmer gently until suds form. You might consider providing finger-bowls full of soapwort suds to friends after serving a meal of wild things.

Just as you would not eat a chunk of soap for fear of the harm it might do to you internally, so likewise you should take care not to ingest soapwort. The saponins could wreak havoc on your digestive tract. While some herbal manuals recommend soapwort as a remedy for several different ailments, the plant is poisonous. Better to use it externally.

Another wild cleanser comes from the yucca plants. Several species of yucca grow prolifically in the desert-dry southwest United States and in Mexico, their native territory. At least one variety *(Yucca filamentosa)* has traveled, through the aid of curious gardeners, toward the Northeast. Here in Virginia I occasionally find fields full of the spiny evergreen plants, where one introduced yucca apparently sent out seedlings year after year. In midsummer, yuccas shoot up a dramatic single flower stalk, topped with white bell flowers at a height of three feet or more. The yucca is a plant you can't miss for its striking appearance—and a plant you ought not to miss for its usefulness.

The Indians in the Southwest who lived around yuccas found many uses for them. Unlike soapwort, the yucca is safe for eating, and we have accounts of Indians who ate both flower and fruit. The flowers are perhaps the most appetizing: crisp white petals, tasting salad green with a hint of floral sweetness. The oval seedpods, picked fresh, were pitted and dried and carried for trail food by traveling Indians. Those who stayed home often ground dried pods into meal.

While seeds and flowers offer food, the long, deep taproot of a yucca offers a fine shampoo. Slip your shovel deep down in beside the spreading foliage. The root grows deep, so it will probably snap off as you lift up. One good-sized chunk, say two inches across and six inches long, will provide one shampoo. Cut the scrubbed root into small chunks and slivers. Boil them in water, three cups to each cup of root chips you use. Suds will rise and the kitchen will smell like something between soap and potato. Boil the mixture gently until two-thirds of the water has evaporated. Now soap makes up a good proportion of the liquid remaining: yucca shampoo. This wild shampoo won't lather like shampoos we are used to, but it will clean hair. Mix equal parts of yucca solution and castile soap if you want more suds.

Many other wild things can help cleanse you too. Cleavers, wild strawberry leaves, the sorrels, yarrow, amaranth, self-heal, and sumac all are natural astringents, meaning that they tend to shrink openings in human tissue and reduce secretions. Teas brewed from these herbs will help wash oily or troubled skin. The mints are delightful additions to bathwater and very gentle on the skin. Just brew a strong cup of tea, then dump it into a hot tub. On a summer's day, when all you need is to rinse off the sweat, a cool mint bath might be the perfect rejuvenator. And for those other days when body or hair needs a real cleaning, try soapwort and yucca, wild and clean.

Purslane

Two hundred years ago, American settlers were sowing seed of purslane. Once summer blew hot, they scattered black seed specks garnered from earlier gardens. The seeds germinated quickly into networks of succulent stems, closely matting the earth. Flat oval leaves, then tiny yellow flowers grew at ground level too. Pea-sized seedpods, left to shatter, would spill out forty or fifty specks into the soil. But colonists certainly gathered in the purslane before it spread.

Purslane came originally from India. Colonists probably brought with them seed stock that had first come to Europe along trade routes from the East. In the 1940s, Mahatma Gandhi named purslane among thirty vegetables suitable for his fellow Indians to cultivate. In such home-grown produce he saw the promise of national self-reliance and an end to hunger among the masses. What a contrast with today's America, currently land of plenty. Few here recognize purslane when they see it. Some even count it an obnoxious weed.

No one is sowing purslane on this continent these days, but the

Portulaca oleracea

plant still remains. It needs a clearing, since it cannot compete with tall, thick weeds. Garden spaces invite its growing. Purslane likes it hot, so it grows thicker stems and spreads a wider network in areas with longer growing seasons. I've seen purslane stems an inch thick in California, but in the Virginia mountains they don't get half that size.

I gather purslane greens from their earliest appearance in the summer until they succumb to the coming of fall. Raw sprigs, stems and leaves, taste crisp and green. A whole salad can center around them, like this Wild Cole Slaw. Gather and chop coarsely 1 cup of purslane greens. Add 1 cup of chopped cabbage and carrot. Also dice in 5 wild garlic bulbs and greens or a single onion. I like to include other chopped greens too, like lamb's quarters, wood sorrel, or sheep sorrel. Seeds season a slaw well too: try wild amaranth or lamb's quarters seeds, caraway or poppy. Toss the salad in a dressing of ¼ cup yogurt, ¼ cup mayonnaise, 3 tablespoons lemon juice, and pinches of yarrow herb, dry mustard, salt, and cayenne pepper. Or simply add some purslane greens to your own cole slaw recipe. They add color and nutrients.

Like so many wild greens, purslane offers vitamins and minerals comparable to or exceeding those of valued garden vegetables. Compare purslane with the cabbage in slaw. According to figures offered by Euell Gibbons, the plants almost equal each other in high water content. But purslane has fewer calories, over twice the calcium, almost ten times the iron, and almost twenty times the vitamin A found in garden-grown cabbage. Only in vitamin C does cabbage exceed purslane, two to one. So a salad of cabbage and purslane gives a well-rounded dish of vitamins and minerals in plenty.

Purslane's high water content and pleasing design make for pretty pickling. Follow any recipe, sweet or dill, using stalks of purslane instead of cucumbers. Or you can use leaves and stems for a relish I call Purslane Piccalilli. Combine in a stainless-steel pan 3 cups of purslane leaves and stems, a dozen wild garlic cloves or a thinly sliced onion, and pickling spices (see "Wild Spice"). Bring to a boil 1 cup vinegar and 1 cup sugar or ½ cup honey, being sure that the sweet is thoroughly dissolved. Pour the boiling syrup over the greens, then quickly bring them to a boil again. Pour into sterilized jars and seal. If you don't want to can the pickles, you can just set the jar in the back of the refrigerator for a few weeks before tasting.

Even if you keep purslane trim by using the greens, some swatches will jump to seed. Those who cultivated purslane must have pulled up plants before the seedpods opened. If you watch the plant in cycle, you'll see inconspicuous dots of yellow blooming along the stems. Today's bloom becomes tomorrow's seedpod: an elfin pouch with a closely fitting cap. The round pod browns and falls open, releasing tiny black seeds. Pull up purslane when the pods are still green and toss the plants on a sheet or newspaper. Within a week the seeds scatter, easy to separate from the withering greens. Use purslane seeds as you might use poppy seeds. Sprinkle them on baked goods, in salad dressings, or on top of a casserole. Or use the seeds as the settlers did: to grow more purslane.

May Apples

WANDERERS of the eastern forests welcome an occasional cool green patch of may apples. Small biennial plants unfold umbrella leaves. One leaf develops in the first year, a forking pair of leaves in the second. Usually the plants cluster at the base of oak and hickory trees, their foliage spreading open like a green canopy a foot above the forest floor.

The month of May will see them flower. From the crook of each two-leafed plant bobs a waxy white bloom. Over the summer, the May flower yields to an August apple. Only its roundness relates it to an apple, though. Plum-sized and lemon-yellow, a single ripe may apple fruit dangles beneath each pair of protective leaves. Peek under at the right time of year and the may apple fruit will drop right into your hand. It will feel soft and smell acid-sweet. To most palates, it is delicious: mild and tart and quite inviting.

I find it hard to resist the temptation of tasting this woodland fruit whenever I find it ripe. But I always go back to perennial patches, hoping to gather enough to cook up May Apple Marmalade. Half a gallon of the fruits is enough. Simmer them, with a little water added, until the fruits soften, then strain them through a food mill or sieve to make a pulp. Adding an equal amount of sugar (or somewhat less honey), this sweet fruit filling can be used in a standard jelly recipe or—if you feel like experimenting—to make a pudding or pie.

Warnings must accompany praises for this woodland delicacy. For, while the fruits are delectable, other parts of the plant could be dangerous. The slender, knotty rootstock and the bright green foliage contain poisons strong enough to kill. As with poke, may apple rootstock contains a toxic substance that inhibits cell growth. Colonists found native Americans using the roots to cure cancers, expel worms, and induce a general catharsis of their internal systems. One investigator also learned of an Indian woman, however, who used the root to commit suicide. Native Americans knew, and we must recognize, the

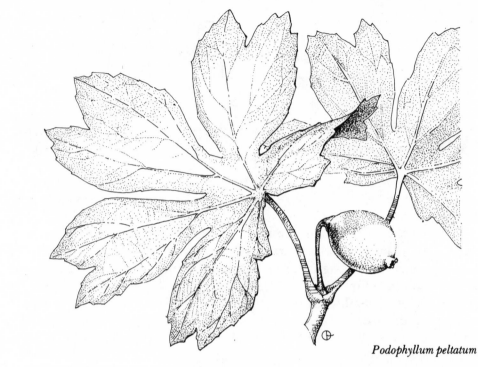

Podophyllum peltatum

potency and the dangers inherent in this lovely woodland character.

And yet, as also with poke, the same toxic ingredients can be put to effective medical use if extracted carefully and administered in tiny doses. Once again, modern science is discovering its own uses for plants gathered by American natives centuries back. The properly prepared active substance in the may apple, called "podophyllotoxin," interrupts cell production by affecting RNA and DNA synthesis directly, according to scientific study over the last twenty-five years. Modern chemical laboratories use and experiment with may apple derivatives daily, and doctors currently use podophyllotoxin preparations to supplement radiation treatment of cancer. Botanical researchers are just now beginning to consider how may apples might be propagated, anticipating that the future need for may apple rootstock may actually exceed the supply that grows wild.

And still the lovely may apple adorns our shady woods. Its

springtime bloom is a favorite sight for many a wildflower fancier. Its sweet yellow fruit makes a woodland forage in late summer worthwhile. And, beneath the ground, secretly, may apple rootstock twists and grows each year: a potent killer and potential healer for modern humankind.

Amaranth

THE European conquest of the Americas affected the lives of many people, many cultures—and many plants. Amaranth was a favored crop among native Americans, a staple grain in the Aztec diet. The stalks grew taller than the men and women who planted them and were topped with dense seedhead bouquets. Anthropologists have found caches of amaranth seed stored centuries ago, leading them to consider it the first North American grain crop. On one dig near Albuquerque, a hundred seeds were found, their age projected back almost seven thousand years. Gathering amaranth seeds, we reach toward the source of much that makes us human.

So common and yet so highly revered was the amaranth that it played a role in Indian religious life. Human effigies were sculpted of amaranth paste, held high in procession, then crumbled into many pieces and solemnly eaten by supplicants. The ritual shares a pattern found in Christian communion as well: by exalting the grain of the earth, we confirm unity with the spirits of nature and partake in the cycles of death and rebirth.

But invading Spaniards considered Indian rituals idolatrous parodies of their own sacred practice. During the Renaissance, amaranth had acquired the mythic reputation of granting everlasting life. The very word "amaranth" comes from the Greek for "deathless" or "unfading," so the Spaniards may have reacted even more fiercely against the sacred plant. They destroyed the Indians, their temples, and their gods. They tried to destroy the amaranth too. But the plant kept on growing, spreading untended throughout South and North America. The invaders simply transformed it from a staple to a weed.

Seeds spread, breeds intermixed. Now some thirty-odd species of amaranth bloom around the world, over twenty of them on this continent. From the prickly, recumbent *Amaranthus cruentus* to the tall, proud, benign *retroflexus* species, many amaranths make themselves at home nearby. They seem to gravitate toward humanity. Clear out a garden plot and let it go to weeds: chances are good that amaranth will appear.

The seedlings push up in early summer. Their friendly leaves feel like thin chamois. Growing in an alternating pattern from a stalk that becomes striated with age, the leaves are tender and sweet early in their growing season. Eaten raw or briefly steamed, they taste quite good. These greens offer remarkably high amounts of calcium, phosphorus, iron, and potassium, and compare favorably with many vegetables in vitamins A and C as well. Since the mature plants will crowd out garden vegetables, I try to gather young seedlings and add them to our early summer dinners.

Historically, amaranth has been cultivated not for greens but for its seeds, which offer protein as hardy as that derived from soybeans. Those who cultivate the plant today prefer the light-colored seed of varieties like the *hypochondriacus*, higher in nutrients, lower in fat and fiber than the shiny black seeds set by most wild American amaranths. But even the wild seeds are worth collecting, to scatter atop breads or omelets as one might use poppy seeds.

Gather amaranth grain when seedheads begin to shatter, usually by late summer. The easiest way to separate seed from stalk is to cut the ripe plant at ground level, put it head first into a paper bag, and let it dry for about a week. Then hold the bag by the neck and shake. Seeds and chaff will scatter. You can thresh the contained seedhead against a tree or cupboard, echoing the movements of peasant women through the ages. Pour the dislodged material onto a platter, then use your breath or a gentle fan to blow away the straw and leaves. And if a little chaff remains, why worry? You've mingled amaranth herb with the seed.

Amaranthus hypochondriacus

The Indians ground these tiny seeds into a meal for baking. Always on the lookout for an easier way to do things, I've tried adding whole seeds to bread recipes. They blend right in and add their own nutrients and nutty flavor. An ancient Indian confection calls for amaranth seed to be popped, then dowsed in honey. You can try this ancient candy too. Heat a tablespoon of oil in a shallow pan, then add a quarter cup of amaranth seed. Keep the temperature under it consistently high and keep the seeds moving. They will crackle with heat, but they won't expand as dramatically as the popcorn we're all used to. Mingle popped amaranth seed with half as much honey, then spread the mixture on waxed paper and let it cool. Now you have a tasty and nutritious snack. Share it in spirit with native Americans from centuries back.

Currently amaranth is a key crop at the Organic Gardening and Farming Research Center in Emmaus, Pennsylvania. Robert Rodale, editor of *Organic Gardening* magazine, and his colleagues consider cultivated amaranth a godsend for home gardeners, hungry Third World nations, and an earth that may have to do with less water, since the plant grows easily, produces voluminously, and can bear a drought. Cultivated varieties from Mexico, Tibet, and elsewhere grow in their experimental plots, and they have sent seed to thousands of home gardeners interested in helping discover the principles of growing amaranth.

With Canadian and American gardens now growing quality amaranth, seeds will spread. I found a fine, tall, white-seeded plant near my back door this summer. A seed must have found its way down from a patch of amaranth planted the year before, ten minutes' walk up the mountain. Proud amaranth scatters the countryside. Unfading red and gold seedheads flicker in the summer sun: the harvest of centuries, recovered for good.

Kudzu

IF YOU live in the southeast corner of the United States, you already know about kudzu. Aggressive vines creep from fields and embankments up fences, walls, and trees. Its benign-looking trefoil and fruity flowers smother the southern summer landscape. Frost may shrivel its leaves, but an enormous underground root stores up enough energy to boost spring growth to an amazing rate of one foot per day.

Kudzu's prolific growth pattern at first won it admiration and a place on this continent. Originally imported from the Orient, it was prized as an ornamental oddity grown to shade the backyard veranda. By the 1920s and 1930s Southern farmers were raising kudzu for other reasons. Farm animals devoured it, and from it they gained important nutrients. It grew in the poorest of soil, filling in gullies and eroded farmland, replenishing nitrogen to spent acreage. It took hold anywhere and seemed to help roadside and railway embankments, where no other plants would keep the dirt from sliding. Government agents and private enthusiasts set in new kudzu plants by the acre.

But over the last twenty years kudzu has lost favor with the American farmers who once praised it as a wonder plant. Kudzu has become a pest. Hard to control and difficult to eradicate, it weighs down buildings and kills the trees that support it. Thousands of dollars are now spent annually trying to wipe it out. But kudzu has a number of uses, well known it its native lands. Maybe those of us who gather wild things can reduce the threat and improve the reputation of kudzu with a single effort.

The plant was originally imported from Japan, where it grows with less abandon and where tradition appreciates it. Oriental cuisine includes kudzu—not only the leaves and flowers but also, more commonly, the starch extracted from its sizable roots. Not only does the root provide useful nutrients. It has medicinal virtues as well. But no one imported Oriental recipes for kudzu when they imported the plant itself.

Recently an entire book has been published to sing the praises of kudzu. William Shurtleff and Akiko Aoyagi's *The Book of Kudzu* (Autumn Press, 1977) shares with westerners many eastern uses for kudzu. The authors foresee a time when "the South may come to be viewed as a treasure trove bursting with 'white gold' just waiting to be harvested."

Kudzu is most noticeable in midsummer when, amidst its profusion of wide leaves, clusters of fuchsia flowers, shaped something like sweet peas, dangle down. The flowers smell like ripe grapes, and their taste combines the flavors of flower, fruit, and vegetable. Kudzu flowers,

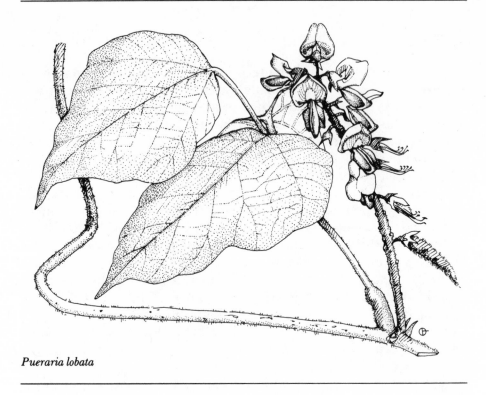

Pueraria lobata

shoots, and tender new leaves are all edible, raw or cooked. But, once the plant has flowered, most of its leaves become too tough to eat, even after lengthy steaming. But mark the spot; because once flowers and foliage die, kudzu roots attain their prime.

Kudzu starch is prepared by a method quite similar to the process used to extract starch from the cattail root (described in "Cattails"). The kudzu root is woodier, though, and fingertips do not so easily dislodge its starches. Dig up a gallon container full of kudzu roots, rinse and scrub them, then get ready for lengthy processing. Occasional attention over several days will provide you with healthful kudzu starch.

Starting with scrubbed medium-size roots (up to an inch and a half across), slice coin-shaped chunks. If you have a blender, fill it halfway with water and add the kudzu chunks a few at a time. Whiz them in the blender, and froth will rise as if you were whipping cream. The new food processors might manage kudzu well. If you have a mill or meat grinder, put smaller chunks of root through. If you are following this recipe on your own resources, dice the roots fine and toss them into clean water.

The extracting process, which runs over several days, requires that you add water, strain the fiber through a fine cloth, wring the cloth-caught fiber for any remaining starch, then add water to the fiber all over again. Let the starchy liquid sit in a cool place for at least two days. As with the cattail, the starch will sink to the bottom. Pour or ladle off the water, then dilute the starch with clean water once again and let it sit another day or two in the cold. Don't let it freeze. Ultimately you will produce a chunky white starch, tending toward dull brown, settling to the bottom. You can either use the wet starch in soups, breads, or stews, or you can dry it on a baking sheet, in the air or in a very low oven, so that you can store it as dried powder.

Shurtleff and Aoyagi offer many traditional recipes for sauces, soups, desserts, and noodles using kudzu powder. While their recipes assume that you will buy packaged kudzu powder, we may as well gather and prepare our own. Try their Oriental vege-kudzu stew, or try this wild North American variety. Heat 2 tablespoons of oil in a saucepan, then sauté a cup or two of available vegetables in it. Try sunflower potato slices, wild garlic cloves, dried daylily flowers, greens from the yard or the freezer, to supplement the traditional sliced celery, carrots, onions, and mushrooms. Put the vegetables in a bowl for the moment. In the same saucepan, heat up 3 cups of vegetable stock or water, a 2-inch sprig of wild ginger, chopped fine, a tablespoon or so of soy sauce, and ¼ teaspoon salt if you need it. Bring this liquid to a boil. Dissolve 3 teaspoons of kudzu powder in 4 tablespoons of water or use about 4 tablespoons of wet kudzu starch. Stir that into the bubbling stock. Add the cooked vegetables and, for an Oriental flair, about a cup of diced tofu. Let the heat rise to just under a boil. The soup is ready.

I mentioned that kudzu powder seems to offer medicinal qualities as well as good taste and texture in food. Its virtues must come from its extreme alkalinity. Oriental tradition prescribes kudzu root tea for stomach troubles: it soothes acid indigestion. For the tea, gather, dice, and dry the roots on a windowsill or in a very slow oven. Simmer them (perhaps with other healing roots like wild ginger or ginseng) for up to an hour, so they slowly release their powers into water.

If more of us actually pulled up surrounding kudzu, the southeastern landscape might be freed of its burden. Considering the abuse this plant has recently suffered, it could use our help. Many public embankments, once deliberately planted in kudzu, are now deliberately sprayed with herbicides, year after year, to kill the kudzu. Avoid those patches of kudzu which have soaked up either herbicides or engine exhaust fumes—poisons and leads that can do harm. Seek out the more secluded strands of kudzu, creeping into woods and fields and backyards unhindered. Spraying kudzu is just covering one mistake with another. We end up the worse for it, our land ravaged, nothing growing once again. Pulling up kudzu is facing the situation. Gathering kudzu is making the most of it.

Jewelweed vs. Poison Ivy

POISON IVY casts shadow on many an outing into the wild. You roam carefree through the woods, but back home you feel slight irritation on your hands or face. Then you see the bumps. The redness. You feel the itch. It can go on for weeks. And you may never want to wander the woods again.

But I suggest one more outing, this time to find jewelweed. The very name sounds soothing. The plant stands, delicate and tall, always in damp places. Its leaves stay paper thin. Flowers bloom, orange or yellow, tiny cornucopias dangling from the stem. Late summer seedpods pop.

Besides its pleasing plant forms, jewelweed has another quality to recommend it. Its juice seems to share some unexplained sympathy with urushiol, the irritating resin of poison ivy. Used properly, jewelweed can stop a poison ivy itch before it ever gets started.

When you bruise a poison ivy plant, its resin imperceptibly oozes out. If you notice that your skin has been touched, try to find a stand of jewelweed nearby and apply its juices to the exposed area. If jewelweed mingles with poison ivy on your skin before the allergic reaction begins, it can deactivate the poison. No bumps, no redness, no itch. Jewelweed will nip the poison itch of ivy in the bud.

You're still best off avoiding poison ivy. Most woodland wanderers recognize the trailing vine that branches into three-leafed clusters. It covers stone walls and fences, fills in orchards and borders fields. It climbs trees, leaving a twisting trail of inch-thick shaggy sinews that root it to the ground. At the growing ends, thin brown branching tendrils reach for support. Three red shiny leaves unfold in springtime.

Poison oaks and ivies, all botanically interrelated, thrive across the continent. Most widely spread is the common poison ivy *(Rhus radicans)*, whose forms range the gamut from three simple oval leaflets to three oak-like lobed leaves. One poison oak occurs in the Southeast, New Jersey across to Texas *(Rhus toxicodendron);* its Pacific counterpart *(Rhus diversiloba)* grows along the Pacific Coast. Both spread oak-leaf-shaped triplets, the only characteristic they share with oak trees. Disagreements often rumble among botanists and local folks alike over what to call a given three-leaf. If it climbs, it's poison ivy. Poison oaks clump like shrubs. But call it oak or ivy or any other name, all these plants inflict an itch.

Two hundred years ago, doctors thought poison ivy itself might prove a remedy. Knowledgeable Indians are reported to have used the plant medicinally, as a poultice to keep wounds open and as a tea to expel ringworm. Europeans learned of poison ivy from early colonists. The plant so intrigued them that in 1788 and 1792, a French and an English physician each publicly announced their success in using

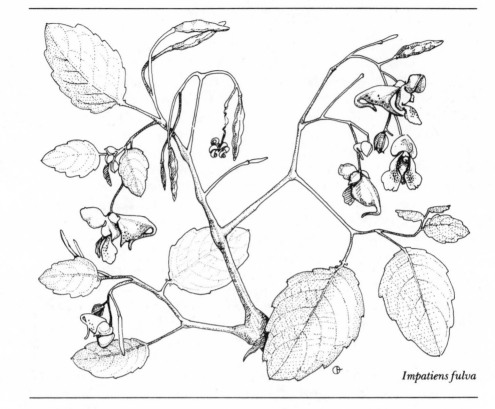

Impatiens fulva

poison ivy to treat chronic dermatitis, "Paralytic Affections and other Diseases of Great Debility," as John Alderson triumphantly described the cure. Most such successes involved an agonizing period of itchy allergic response, after which the patient emerged, thoroughly debilitated, but with the original ailment cured. Thankfully, these practices vanished before the turn of the twentieth century.

Modern medical literature abounds in references to the poison oaks and ivies, considering them the cause of ailments, not the cure. Most articles toss back and forth the virtues of one pharmaceutical treatment versus another, applied once the itch sets in. Most make the sensible suggestion to wash one's hands (and any other body parts that touched the ivy) with soap and water after a walk. Most people can combine this practice with spot applications of jewelweed on the trail to avoid the itch completely.

Those of us who live from Newfoundland to Saskatchewan, south and west to Oklahoma, can go hunting for jewelweed. Walking up the mountain in Virginia, I pass by large stands of jewelweed wherever stream meets path. I crush succulent young stems in springtime, soft leaves in summer. Then I smear the handful of juicy greenery over hands and face and feel safer as I walk through shrubs toward trees.

If I notice that I've mingled with poison ivy, I seek out jewelweed in wet woods, streambeds, full-sun swamps, or in between. In early spring, the primary leaves look almost square. Warmth elongates the stems, upward to six feet by full summer. Mature leaves turn oval, scalloped, delicate, flat, thin. Watery, hollow green stalks sink down into a red root bundle. Deer enjoy the lacy tops of jewelweed. I've found whole patches cropped.

Every part of the jewelweed plant activates against the ivy poison. Just-flowering tops are most potent and most beautiful. Carry home a bouquet of jewelweed, and you can take a fragrant therapeutic bath. A simple tea is made with the flowering herb: four cups of boiling water poured over a cup of fresh jewelweed, left to steep about fifteen minutes. Pour the pot of amber tea into bath water and enjoy a floral bath that soothes.

The same tea can be frozen in cubes, as Euell Gibbons suggests. Jewelweed ice cubes help most in winter and early spring, when urushiol oozes out of hairy roots and red bud tips but jewelweed still lies low. Simply let a pot of strong jewelweed tea sit covered until it is cool, then strain it into a ice-cube tray. Erbin drops a flower into each cube to remember summer's bloom. These ice cubes are the only way we have to preserve the soothing strength of jewelweed, since standing tea and dried herb seem to lose that virtue.

I suppose that when medical researchers finally put their minds to it they will invent a poison ivy ointment with jewelweed as its base, available at the corner drugstore. For those who live in the cities or on the West Coast, the cure will finally be yours too. But if I'm still in the country where jewelweed grows, I'll still go out and pick it. Someday they may put jewelweed in ointment, but they can't put flowers in a tube.

Summer Smoke

DRIVING along the highways on these hot summer days, you can't miss mullein. Tall single stalks rise one to six feet in the air, sporting bright yellow flowers. Mullein seems to favor the easy growing grounds of highway embankments and flat pastureland. All across the continent, as a matter of fact, bright stands of mullein ornament roads and byways. But, if you're out to gather mullein, keep off the beaten track. Dangerous amounts of lead land on plants growing near the road. Take your search away from the steaming asphalt into cooler pastures.

Look for mullein's long, furry, white-green leaves radiating from a single center. Look too for the distinctive flower stalk, often branching into a candelabrum of six or eight clustered flower heads. They shoot straight up, brightly lit with sunshine yellow.

Mullein has a long history. Some old-timers call it Indian tobacco, raising a vision of primeval days before Sir Walter Raleigh and the tobacco boom. Others call it rabbit ears, for the shape and texture of its leaves. Most of them remember smoking mullein as kids out behind the barn before they could get hold of the real stuff.

But old herbal books consider mullein more than just juvenile tobacco. They name it as a cure for throat ailments. If you have a smoker's cough, they suggest, smoke mullein to soothe the pain. This claim may go too far. Smoking anything will irritate the throat. But smoking gathered mullein, picked in fields nearby, is a step toward health away from winston, salem, and pall mall.

You may either pick an entire plant, clipping the thick stalk near the ground, or pluck a few leaves to dry and sample. If you cut the whole plant, hang it upside down in a dark, breezy place to dry. Dry single leaves by spreading them out on a clean screen or unfolded newspaper. Lay them out flat, no one touching another. Let them get lots of air but no sun. In a week or two, depending on humidity, the

Verbascum thapsus

leaves should be crumbly dry and ready to smoke. Pulverize them between your palms to simplify rolling the herb up in cigarette papers. Store the rest in an airtight jar on a dark shelf for a year-round natural smoke.

Mullein alone is a gentle smoke, only mildly aromatic. I like to blend a Good Smoke, using mullein as a base and other flavorful herbs in with it: red raspberry leaves, yarrow, self-heal. Catnip and pennyroyal add natural menthol. A pinch of camomile sweetens the smoke. Red clover flowers add a sweet, grassy flavor. Ginseng leaves add mystery.

We have all been led to believe that smoking means tobacco, cut and blended for us into familiar brands that vary only slightly one from another. In recent years some have learned to smoke a different herb imported from parts south—an herb, by the way, whose harshness can be tempered by the addition of mild mullein just as soda smooths scotch. But this new smoke is just the beginning.

Smoking need not mean fine-blend tobaccos, micronite filters, and getting close on to a dollar a pack. Home-gathered herbs, fresh and flavorful, native to your own environment, can be gathered in season, mixed to taste, and rolled whenever you have the urge. It takes forethought to gather mullein as it blooms. It takes dexterity to roll your own. But put in a little time and effort, and you'll turn out a smoke with character.

AUTUMN

Self-Heal

WHEN I learn of a plant brought to this continent by colonists from Europe, I figure it has a good reason for being here. And when I hear of a plant with names as suggestive as "self-heal," "woundwort," and "heal-all," I figure that the plant has powers. Brought to this country by gardeners and herbalists who knew why it was so named, self-heal took off on its weedy own. Now we have the plant growing wild all around us, coast to coast, its healing properties all but forgotten.

You may notice it in early autumn, one of the last plants to bloom. Purple velvet blossoms encircle a brown seed cob. Their shape recalls the flowers of catnip, spearmint, and other members of the *Labiatae* or Mint family. Lacking fragrance, self-heal still compares with its minty relatives in herbal potency.

The great Renaissance herbalist Gerard praised *Prunella vulgaris*, or self-heal, as one of the best of the "Wound herbes." "The decoction of Prunell made with wine and water," he suggested, "doth join together and make whole and sound all wounds, both inward and outward." Such a description evokes pictures of knights in armor finding herbs on the battlefield, preparing them in rustic goblets, and applying them to sword wounds newly inflicted. But we can put self-heal to more pastoral uses, gathering it as needed for garden cuts and scrapes, drying it for teas and washes throughout the year.

Modern analysis reveals that self-heal is astringent and styptic. It reduces secretions and slows the flow of blood. Wrinkle a fresh leaf of self-heal onto a cut or scratch, and you will see that the bleeding does

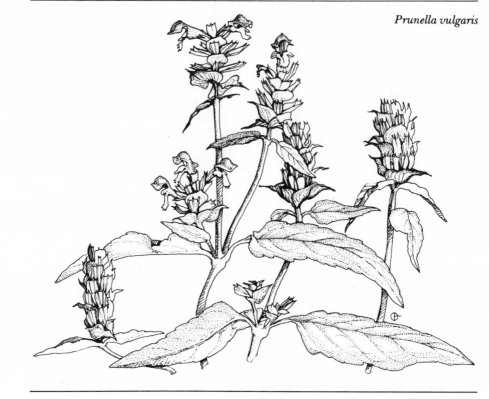

diminish. These properties explain its age-old use against outward wounds and suggest a place for self-heal tea in the bathroom, to wash or rinse one's face after a shave. Brew the tea from fresh leaves as long as you find them growing. Gather a bundle to dry, just as the flowers start to bloom, and save the herb in an airtight jar for winter.

Modern herbals also designate self-heal tea a tonic, like ginseng and yarrow. They say that steady sipping, a cup a day over a long period, will strengthen the body. Its green grassy taste gives one the sure feeling of earth and herbs in abundance.

Self-heal's late blooms are enough to make me appreciate it. Rich purple flowers bedeck fields and forest clearings until serious freezing turns them brown. Its flowers make us notice; its curative powers give us reason to reflect. In the days before band-aids and mercurochrome, people sought out leaves and brewed teas to treat their wounds. There is a moral in the bloom of self-heal: with diligence and knowledge and the help of the green growing world, we can learn to heal ourselves.

Wild Spice

HERBS and spices, what's the difference? You use herbs in an early course: soup, meat, vegetables, eggs, occasionally in a loaf of bread. You more often use spices for dessert: spice cake, baked apples, nutmeg in the pumpkin pie. Or for a special breakfast: waffles or French toast. Herbs taste green and vegetative. Spices taste brown, sweet, and tangy. Herbs are leaves. Spices are berries, bark, or roots. Herbs grow in a temperate region, while spices usually come from the tropics. But our cooler end of the globe grows a few spices of its own: wild spice from North America.

Colonists named wild ginger and wild allspice after tropical spices they already knew (see "Wild Ginger"). Like wild ginger, wild allspice or spicebush (*Benzoin aestivale*) is not related to the plant for which it was named. Allspice (*Pimenta officinalis*) grows in this hemisphere, but in Central America and the West Indies. Both wild allspice and the cinnamon tree, its East Indian relative, belong to the Laurel family. Wild allspice grows on the North American continent, in cooler climes.

Found from Maine and Ontario south to Florida and west to Texas, the wild allspice grows small and bushy in damp, woodsy lands. It is an early bloomer, producing frothy flowers that float like yellow mist in low treetops on early spring days. Allspice flowers are marvelously fragrant, combining flower sweet and spicy tingle. Allspice's flat oval leaves smell good too. Sometimes, charging through the woods, I am

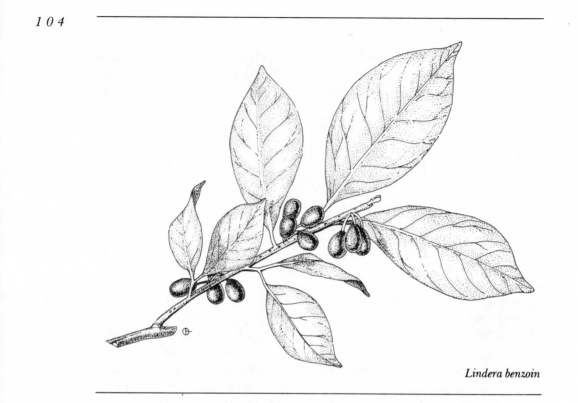

Lindera benzoin

stopped short. I swoon in the odor effusing from bruised spicebush leaves. Even in winter depths you might see a bush with speckled wood, light brown in color. Scratch the bark surface, peel off a curl. The smell will tell you that you've found wild allspice.

You can imagine what a good tea wild allspice makes. As with sassafras, the leaves are almost too strong, unless very new and tender, to brew into a tea. But outer bark shavings and budding twig ends make an aromatic brew. Let the woody parts simmer gently half an hour, as you might do with twigs of sweet birch.

Now that it's fall, wild allspice berries glow red while leaves are turning yellow. When colonists named the plant after tropical allspice, they must have been using the berries for spicing, ground or whole. They gleam bright and tempting, but eating whole berries of allspice could be dangerous. Equally harmful would be a mouthful of tropical allspice or whole nutmeg too. If it is used whole in pickling for flavor and color but not for eating, wild allspice is safe. The berries smell good and strong, but few would want a mouthful of them anyway.

Here's a simple recipe for using up those summer squashes that keep on producing while spicebush berries turn red. Slice small zucchini or yellow summer squashes to fill sterile pint jars. Blend a sweet pickle brine of apple cider vinegar and sugar, proportioned two to one. Place raw squash slices in a jar, then toss in about a dozen wild allspice berries. Pour the boiling pickle syrup over the squash and berries, then seal up the jar. The berries will lose their bright red, but they will impart to the squash a subtle spice from the wild.

Many other wild things gathered throughout the year make for good pickling spices. Sassafras root bark shavings, added to the brine before boiling or added to the pickle jar itself, give pickles a zing. Wild ginger root is a favorite pickling spice of mine. You may not want to retire your favorite imports—cinnamon, nutmeg, or tropical allspice—from the kitchen cabinet. But you may want to add some wild spice to your cuisine.

Chicory

CHICORY makes me happy. Its flowers mirror the sky. On days when I get outside before the sun starts blistering, I catch the flowers open. A field shines blue. I remember my mother singing, driving to Silver Lake on a summer's day. "Chickery chick, cha-la, cha-la," my memory echoes, and I feel happy.

Only recently have I learned to use chicory. Flowers may make me glad, but leaves and roots bring out the industry in me. In spring I seek blanched, tender chicory greens for salads and for cooking. In fall I dig up roots. And as winter arrives, I keep a few roots protected to force spring sprouts before their time (see "Winter Sprouts"). My life entangles more intimately with chicory's cycles of green growth, and its flowers make me all the more happy.

In Europe, chicory is cultivated, cherished for greens and hardy root both. Over here, one occasionally finds cultivated chicory at the greengrocer's, or chicory seeds for sale in a catalog. They will produce a plumper plant than those growing in fields and on roadsides, but similar in green taste and nutrients to its wild relation. Several coffee companies enrich their morning beverage with ground roast chicory root. Ironically, much if not all of the chicory now included in American coffee brands has been imported from European chicory growers. With all the blue that lines our highways in summer, you would think we could harvest our own.

A relative of the dandelion (they are both in the Composite or Daisy family), chicory sends down a similarly long, thick root to tap minerals from deep within the soil. It sends up a flower stalk perennially. Greens should be gathered early on in its growing, before any stalk appears, and can be cooked or eaten raw for salad. Roots should be gathered late, after the flowers have died. Often one can gather both at the same time, since autumn sunshine sometimes coaxes out new leaves at the base of a spent flower stalk.

When you gather chicory roots, go prepared for serious digging. The ground around here is rather rocky, and rarely have I managed to unearth an entire chicory root, top to toe. They usually snap off at about the level my shovel reaches, leaving me with an eight- or ten-inch section. The roots are tough, almost woody. They don't appeal to me for eating, although they are quite safe, boiled until soft.

To make the chicory hot drink one must roast the gathered roots. Gather plenty, because their volume shrinks surprisingly as you process them. Once home, trim off all above-ground parts and scrub the chicory roots well. Cut them with a sharp knife or pruning clippers into one-inch sections and roast them in a slow oven (no hotter than 300 degrees F., 150 degrees C.) for about an hour, maybe less. Keep an eye on them: you need to see that they brown but don't char. The inner

Cichorium intybus

core, white when you gather them, should turn a toasty color. You will smell the sweet aroma as the roots roast.

I put the roast root sections into my blender to grind them. Others may have coffee grinders that will do the trick, although they may require pieces cut smaller than one inch long. Roast chicory root is a mottled brown color, lusty rich in aroma, and can be ground coarse or fine. It can be brewed like coffee on its own or mixed with roast dandelion root, prepared similarly. Or, of course, it can be added to coffee to make a richer, darker, and more healthful brew. Chicory can stretch your coffee and sweeten its acidity. I no longer brew coffee without it.

I've met people with a definite prejudice against chicory coffee. It all goes back to the last world war, I believe, when chicory augmented expensive and limited coffee imports. People began to associate chicory with deprivation and poverty. But put the whole picture together—roots for drinking, greens for health, and flowers for summer cheer. Chicory seems a plant of plenty.

Autumn Teas

A UTUMN weather can ask a lot of one's body. The wind blows, the temperature shifts, and even when the sun shines, the air feels cold. Colds come on with a vengeance. One feels vulnerable. But, as so often, nature provides. Green leaves still grow as summer turns to autumn, many of them the ideal herbs for teas to keep one healthy.

Many potent brewing herbs that bloomed in summer still send out volunteers as autumn draws near. Red clover, yarrow, self-heal still bloom here and there, less potent than their summer predecessors, yet offering fresh sustenance for the searcher. Each of these herbs has its power to heal and sustain. Each offers autumnal healthfulness.

Most mints are beyond blooming, but even they continue to send out leaves with the pungent aroma that suggests their herbal powers. The mints that you gather for drying to make wintertime teas should be those that blossom at the start of the season. But as long as mint

greens stand, you may as well gather them. Your winter cache will last that much longer. Collect a few extra leaves for the pot, since their potency is reduced by cooler temperatures and frost at night.

The plants whose leaves you gathered for teas back in early springtime have by now grown their full course. They were fresh and green in spring, then they waned in the heat of summer. Now they thrive, green and hardy, awaiting winter cold. Strawberry leaves, in warmer climates, are almost evergreen. Violet leaves die back, but they usually offer a light crop before the frost hits them. Dandelion leaves, a healthy addition to any pot of tea, return to springtime sweetness once their flowering cycle ends.

We brew teas in order to express an herb's essential ingredients from leaf into water. Many of these wild herbs take their character from volatile oils; many provide vitamins, if we take the care to catch them. Since both the oils and the vitamins will escape in air, herbal teas should be brewed with care and attention. Use a teapot or a closely covered pan. Use 2 or 3 teaspoons of fresh leaves per teacup, 1 or 2 teaspoons of dried herb. Bruise fresh leaves as you put them in the pot, to release their oils. Pour over the herb fresh boiling water, a little over a cup for each cup of tea. Cover and steep about five minutes. Never boil an herb tea. The same recipe holds for almost every tea concocted of leaves or flowers, officially called an "infusion." The process soon becomes second nature.

Teas made from roots and bark require different treatment— "decoction" rather than "infusion"—to express less-accessible principles from the woody plant parts. So a tea made of sassafras root bark or wild ginger root requires boiling, not simply dowsing the roots with boiling water. Here two teaspoonfuls will brew a strong cup of tea. Toss into a pot of fresh water clean root parts, bark shavings, or twigs. They need not be broken up. Bring the pot to a boil, then let it bubble gently for ten to thirty minutes. Brewing time depends on the character, potency, and freshness of the plant part you've gathered. Since the taste of teas made from roots and bark does not depend on elusive volatile oils or vitamins, they can sit on the stove or in the refrigerator. Many, like sassafras, can even be brewed over and over again.

Herbal teas are year-round pleasures. Once you begin to brew them at home, you'll wonder how the majority of Americans stay content, choosing between soda pop, coffee, and orange pekoe. Even the thought of a warm green drink, devoid of sugar or caffeine, calms me. Winter is coming, a time when herbs duck underground and we must count on those we dried over summer. But there is yet time to take one more walk through fields and yards, gathering what comes to view for a last pot of fresh herb tea. A few sprigs of yarrow, a stray red clover, a handful of strawberry leaves, and a spray of mint will brew a comforting cup of tea to celebrate the autumn.

Sumac

AMIDST the bright leaves of autumn, sumac shines. It adds its brilliant scarlets to the changing landscape. And after leaves fall and autumn becomes more dreary, moving into winter, sumac seedheads still stand scarlet and bright.

Several varieties of sumac grow in clearings and along roadways throughout the United States and Canada. Single-stalked shrubs, often growing in clusters, stretch from three to twenty feet high. The staghorn sumac is known for its fuzziness; the smooth sumac looks similar, although bark and berries grow smooth. The dwarf sumac and the squaw bush, eastern and western varieties, run smaller. And yet all these common plants share that characteristic bright red cluster of berries, formed in early autumn and carried on through winter.

Some people balk at the idea of gathering sumac, having heard about poison sumac somewhere along the way. And indeed a poisonous sumac does exist. But it is rarely found, and then only in swampy places. Its berries hang down like a bunch of grapes, separate and white—quite different in appearance from the safe red sumac clusters. If you ever discover a bush with leaf structure similar to the familiar sumacs and with white berries, avoid touching it. It causes extreme skin irritation, more serious than poison oak or poison ivy.

But red-berried sumacs all are safe, useful, and appealing. Many Indian tribes used the berries, as well as roots, bark, and leaves, in medicinal preparations, to cure ailments as diverse as venereal disease and a sore throat. The most common medicinal use of sumac berries, by American natives and newcomers alike, has been as a gargle. The acid astringency of sumac tea cleanses one's throat and mouth with a flavor more pleasing than any mouthwash bought in a store.

To make up a sumac gargle, gather ripe berries as early as possible, coax them off the stem, and steep them in boiling water, about four cups water to a cup of sumac seed. The tea will turn deep red. Strain it through a couple of layers of cheesecloth to extract seeds and hairs.

Rhus glabra

Then keep it in your medicine chest—it won't go bad—for daily use as a wild mouthwash.

By adding a little sweetness to the recipe, you can make a refreshing drink. Many compare sumac tea to pink lemonade because of its acid flavor and warm red color. Follow the directions above to steep a tea of sumac seed, then add sugar, honey or sorghum to taste. Let the tea cool and serve it over ice. Sumac berries add zest to hot teas too. They can be gathered on into the season, but autumn elements drain their flavor and vitamin content. It is probably best to gather sumac berries now while they are bright and fresh. Make up a pitcher of wild sumac tea for a taste of Indian summer.

Watercress

S UPERMARKETS sell it for a preposterous price per pound. Vitamin manufacturers cultivate it for nutritious riches. European settlers brought it over here, and now it has gone wild. Yet we usually think of it as a high-class delicacy: watercress sandwiches, white bread with trimmed crusts, daintily spread with butter. But there are so many hearty ways to use watercress, and so many good reasons to do so.

It grows out there in shallow streams and brooklets, fresh for picking through many months of the year. Spring watercress is cool and tender. Summer watercress tastes hot. But, when most greens have died back and the harvest feels finished, autumn watercress returns to palatability. Water flowing past its roots keeps foliage alive. Only an icy freeze or smothering snow will kill it until spring thaw brings it back to life.

When you find an accessible watercress patch, investigate the path its water travels before it feeds the cress. Serious illness can result from eating watercress grown in polluted water. If cows graze upstream, using the spring as their wallow, dangerous bacteria may invade the leaves. Your county agent may be able to determine the safety of nearby streams if you are concerned. But, once you've verified the safety of your cress, you can eat it with gusto.

Most people enjoy watercress in a salad, as long as it mixes with other greens that taste cooler. Chickweed (see "Winter Greens") blends well with watercress in its color, flavor, texture, and the time of year it ripens. You can gather them together throughout warm spells in winter to make a simple Winter Green Salad. Chop chickweed, watercress, and wild garlic cloves into manageable pieces. Mix up a simple vinaigrette, with three parts oil to one part vinegar, a dash of salt, lemon juice, dry mustard, and cayenne pepper. Shake, pour, toss, serve. This salad is incredibly nutritious.

Or you can cook the same greens together. Chop them as for the raw salad. Soften the garlic in a skillet with melted butter or cooking oil, then quickly turn in the greens, stirring constantly. Pungent seeds or almond slivers dress the dish. Cook these greens very little, though, particularly since vitamins escape with the steam.

Watercress lines many a sandwich well—not just the country club kind, but also a healthy cheese, sprout, and watercress sandwich— mayo on one side, mustard on the other, mmmm. That might be one of the healthiest lunches you could prescribe. The cheese and sprouts offer protein, and the sprouts and cress offer vitamins and minerals abounding, particularly since both come fresh and still alive.

Watercress soup steams warm and nutritious. Watercress soufflé rises light and green. You can make either from this recipe. Melt 2 tablespoons butter, add an onion, wild garlic cloves, basil and sage. Once the herbs have imparted their flavor to the butter, remove and save them. To the flavored butter add 2 more tablespoons butter and ½ teaspoon salt. Turn the heat up under it until it sizzles. Immediately add 1 cup milk, ¾ cup grated cheese (a mild white cheese works best), and 3 beaten egg yolks. Stir them over low heat and the sauce will thicken. Once it is good and thick, stir in 2 cups chopped watercress and the onion and garlic you set aside. To make a soufflé, fold in 3 stiffly beaten egg whites, slide the mixture into a greased casserole, and bake about 30 minutes at 375 degrees. To make soup, add to your sauce enough water, stock, or milk to give it the right consistency. Watercress adds nutrients and character to any other soup you make as well.

I can even imagine chopping watercress to sprinkle on baked potatoes or into muffin batter. One can dry watercress herb (just before flowering, hang or spread it in a dark, breezy place) and sprinkle watercress flakes on any dish imaginable. My fancy flies as I

Nasturtium officinale

think of more ways to use watercress. It's growing out there, in abundance, full of nutrients, waiting to be had. Some seed companies sell watercress. It is easy to germinate and grow, provided you have a shallow clean pool or stream into which you can set the seedlings. Vitamin companies cultivate watercress as a natural source of vitamin A, but it also provides B and C vitamins and many minerals as well—iron, copper, phosphorus, magnesium, manganese, and calcium.

I must caution you that one herbalist, John Lust in *The Herb Book* (Bantam, 1974), warns against excessive consumption of watercress. He grants it magnificently effective for gout, digestion, and a phlegm-filled throat, useful against anemia and eczema. He finds that its rich nutrients stimulate glandular activity and provide enough vitamin C to prevent illness. But he writes, "It should not be taken daily and no longer than four weeks even with interruptions." Now "it" means watercress tea or watercress juice drunk straight—not watercress leaves mingled in your diet. But excessive amounts of watercress could lead to kidney ailments. So be forewarned and plan to gather watercress in the light of your own health. Watercress as a daily garnish will probably benefit you, while an exclusive diet of watercress might not.

Many free and nutritious weeds have earned a bad reputation, but watercress never lost the respect that it deserves. Called *Nasturtium officinale,* it was an "official" medicinal herb. Like asparagus, dandelion, jasmine, hyssop, lavender, and other plants, watercress won from Renaissance botanists the Latinate mark of distinction as a valuable herb. Today most people know watercress, but only as a high-priced item stocked next to lettuce in the supermarket. You may see more watercress in the supermarket than you see in untouched springs—but that only speaks for where you spend your time, not where the watercress is growing.

Puffballs

SOMETIMES a child will find, in field or forest, a little white globe. She picks it up, pinches it, poof! A gentle spray of mouse-brown dust. Puffball spores disperse like smoke or fairy glitter.

But to the autumn forager puffball spores mean edible mushrooms discovered too late for the eating. For when puffballs poof, they have already passed through their cycle of fruition. They send out spores, like seeds, for the new year's crop. Arrive a week or a month earlier, and you will be able to gather puffballs. From spring through autumn, whenever moisture conditions are right, puffballs appear. Along with

Lycoperdon perlatum

morels, they are the most positively identifiable edible mushrooms around.

Puffballs pop up bright white, in rich cleared pastureland or on the rotting limbs of fallen trees. Orson K. Miller's excellent guidebook, *Mushrooms of North America* (Dutton, 1978), names sixteen species. All form round white globes with hardly a stem to stand on. They feel soft and spongy, like any other mushroom. Some species fruit no larger than an apricot, while others grow as large as a melon. Age turns them brown and warty. Then a hole cracks open on top, through which the spores scatter. Mycelium (a fungus's underground root system) may remain where you find a spent puffball. Come back next summer or next autumn.

Of those sixteen species, it's easy to separate the good puffballs from the four varieties that might be bitter to the palate. If a puffball is white through and through, smells good, and is big enough to bother with, you can gather it to eat. One must also always check to find the flesh uniform and patternless. Be sure you do not see the embryo of mushroom stem or gills. If you do, you may be gathering Amanita buttons and they may be deadly. Careful observation should guide you as you gather and prepare puffballs. Slice each puffball at least once down the middle to verify white uniformity. You can peel off the outer skin if it feels tough.

Puffballs can be sautéed cr deep fried, or dipped in a tempura batter. For simplicity's sake, I prefer a Wild Puffball Fry. Fill a small paper bag with one cup of flour (half white, half whole wheat) and half a teaspoon of salt. Pinch in some dried herb, if you want seasoning. Toss in manageable slices of fresh white puffball. Shake gently to coat them. Melt 3 to 4 tablespoons of butter in a skillet and fry the fungus until golden brown. Puffballs taste sweet, nutty, earthy.

North American natives gathered puffballs for eating; so did settlers traveling west. And from several tribes explorers learned that dry spores, the smoky dust of puffballs, have hemostatic properties. Indians used the dust to treat bleeding cuts and wounds, and may even have gathered it in autumn to store through the winter for treatment when needed. When I find puffball dust, I like to use it for enchantment. And I'll come back next year, looking for the ripe white fruit before it turns to dust.

Wild Grapes

A COOL day, autumn in Virginia. I stand amidst a forest, its summer greens felled by occasional frosts. I look up through the interwoven network of limbs and vines, and I can see tight clusters of well-formed grapes hanging high. Grape vines cling to straight black limbs. The most luscious fruits reach the highest. Down here, I know how the fox felt.

Last year these grapes grew plump within reach, using abandoned apple trees and healthy locusts as arbors for support. I gathered bucketfuls, enough for lots of fox-grape jelly. Since grapes, particularly the green ones, contain natural pectin, a simple recipe produces successful jelly. First, simmer a covered kettle of fruit over low heat, adding only a half cup of water for each gallon of grapes. After the skins have burst and the juice is flowing, strain the liquid through a colander or jelly bag. Euell Gibbons suggests that one leave wild grape juice sitting overnight, so that any gritty sediment will sink to the bottom. However, much of the juice's vitamin richness will escape if it sits overnight, especially if it is left uncovered.

To sweeten, measure a cup of sugar for each cup of grape juice you have strained, or add half as much honey. (You may need commercial pectin, though, if you use honey.) Put the juice back on the fire and add the sweetening gradually as the juice just starts to boil. Stir it constantly as it boils for up to two minutes. After about a minute and a half of boiling, jelly-test it with a spoon or put a saucerful of jelly in the fridge for a minute to see if it jells. If it doesn't, put it back over the heat, but keep stirring so it doesn't burn. I usually just pour it into sterilized jars after a minute and a half of boiling. If it doesn't jell, I call it wild grape syrup. We have quite a repertoire of wild syrups—failed jellies—in our pantry. They make waffles wilder.

You can make grape jelly out of any grape you find out there, from the deep blue fox grape to the strawberry-blond muscadine. Roaming through an abandoned homestead, one occasionally finds Concord grape vines gone wild. Grapes growing in field or forest could be one of more than twenty species native to this land. Grapes grow in almost every North American climate, preferring the sunny edge of a northern forest. All species share wide, heart-shaped leaves, often complicated with two more points on either side of center. The leaves are commonly furry, their edges always jagged. Grapes climb with curling tendrils, thick vines often swinging ten, twenty, thirty feet up. After the leaves fall, tendrils and fruit clusters still frame the landscape à l'art nouveau.

One must beware of a poisonous look-alike of wild grape: the Canada moonseed. Its berries may look appealing but could be harmful spread on toast. They do taste bad, though, and the plant's

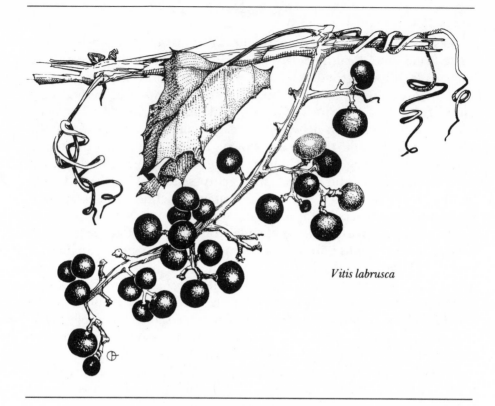

Vitis labrusca

formation does not exactly replicate that of the wild grape. Moonseed leaves have smooth edges and the vine climbs by twining, not by sending out branching tendrils. The seed for which the plant is named also distinguishes it. Shaped like a crescent moon, the single moonseed contrasts with the multiple pear-shaped seeds found in each edible grape.

   If you find a few gallons of good-tasting grapes, you can make wild wine with them. I made some last year, but I seem to have skimped on the sugar. It has the body of a red burgundy but tastes too tart. If I were doing it again, I would make it like this: gather a gallon of ripe, sweet grapes. Some wild grapes taste better than others; discriminate before you pick them. Put them in a three- to five-gallon crock and mash them with a wooden spoon or clean fingers to get the juice flowing. Add a gallon of water. Let it sit, covered, for three days, stirring a little each day. Strain out skins and seeds, then add to the juice 5 pounds sugar for your gallon of grapes. Let that sit, covered, stirring once a day, for a week. Then strain and pour into sterile screw-top bottles, leaving the tops less than tight. In about a month you'll hear that the fizz and fermentation have stopped. Tighten the lids and wait a good six months before you taste it.

I hope that next year's autumn will be wetter and more grapes hang nearby. Then I can make some wine again. This year I can only stand and look at the fruitless vines at eye level and the plump bunches higher up. Grapes appear in cycles, but grape wine lasts all year. I drink it slowly, appreciatively, in years like this one, years of dearth of grapes. I raise my glass to the few wild grapes hanging beyond my reach today, upward to the autumn sun.

Ginseng the Inscrutable

LIGHTNING struck down, so the story goes, and planted ginseng, mingling sky-fire and deep waters in the earth. Emperors of China coveted the magical plant over centuries. Wealthy Oriental warlords wore the root around their necks, an amulet of long life and power.

A European missionary learned of ginseng's healing powers when he lived among the Chinese in the early 1700s. Another missionary, reading his report, began to search the New World for the plant. And finally, in 1716, Father Lafitau found native American ginseng, closely related to the Asian variety, near today's Montreal.

Iroquois Indians helped Lafitau find his ginseng. They knew it as one of hundreds of potent herbs thriving in their forests. Indian names for ginseng, like the Chinese term from which our word derives, meant "human root." To the native American and the Oriental, the occasional resemblance between a ginseng root and the human form signaled special powers: heavenly order planted in the dust of the earth.

European mercenaries soon found out about ginseng. They hired Indians to gather the plunder, paying them 25 cents per pound, then receiving $5 per pound on the Oriental market. Within a few years, thousands of pounds of ginseng were being transported to Shanghai each year. In 1878 alone, 421,395 pounds were exported, valued at almost half a million dollars. Currently one New York herb wholesaler lists native American ginseng at a price approaching $200 per pound.

The root of long life and power made some people very rich along the way. When its magic turned to money, though, the ginseng began its retreat deeper into the woods, away from the humans who were devouring it. Scarcity continues to raise the price ever higher, inspiring ever more extravagant myths. The Chinese legend depicting ginseng climbing out of the ground and ascending into starry heavens seems a portent. Ginseng is disappearing from the earth.

Wild Asian ginseng *(Panax schinseng)* once thrived throughout the mountainous regions of northern China, Korea, and southeastern Russia. It may have grown in the Himalayas too. The Asian native is said to be nearly extinct in the wild today, although more Oriental ginseng is cultivated each year.

The North American variety is threatened as well. Ironically, more Americans than ever before are encountering ginseng these days—meeting it not in the wild but in Chinatown tearooms and hip head shops. So more Americans take off into the woods in search of ginseng, stripping forests indiscriminately of our meager supply.

International herb traders have agreed on certain limits to the collection and sale of wild ginseng. Roots may not be collected before August 15; they may not be traded before September 15. Ginseng has not yet been marked "endangered" by the federal government, but individual states are imposing even more stringent rules on the ginseng market. So far the rules apply to the collection of ginseng for sale, not for personal use. But those of us who recognize ginseng's scarcity as well as its value must accept responsibility for gathering it in season, in moderation, and with concern for the ongoing life of the species. Only public ignorance of the plant has saved it so far; only education and respect can save it for the future.

To save the ginseng, we begin by learning its cycle of life. The root is a tough, white, gnarled, and fleshy carrot, stretching four to six inches underground when the plant is mature. Tendrils branch out from the central root, complicating its design and occasionally suggesting arms and legs. From this perennial root arises a single stem, unfurling in early spring to a mature height of a foot or two. Compounds of five leaves each, joined starlike at a center, stretch out on leaf stalks from that stem.

In late spring ginseng bursts into flower: a delicate globe of blossoms, a white almost green. By late summer berries take shape, and in autumn red fruits fall. The leaves turn yellow earlier than others in the woods. The stalk dies and ginseng retreats underground for another winter.

This yearly cycle repeats itself, in shady forest seclusion, over many years. Knowing the growing cycle of ginseng is just as important as knowing its habitat, for the careful ginseng hunter must know when to look for ginseng as well as where. The potency of the plant rises and falls with the seasons. You want to gather ginseng root when its nutrients have sunk underground. You want to gather it, that is, as the berries fall and leaves wither, early to mid-fall.

As you dig out the root, you can investigate the plant's age more precisely. Each fall, the ginseng sets a bud for next year's growth. Successive buds leave a spiraling pattern of scars on the section joining stem with knobby root. By counting these bud scars, you can discover the exact age of the ginseng you are uprooting. Be sure that it is at least five, even eight years old before disturbing it. Younger roots do not offer full ginseng potency.

Separate the root from its leaf stalk immediately, so disturbed leaves do not draw sustenance from the root, thereby depleting it. Bring the leaves home separate from the root: they make a delicate herb tea. The unearthed root should be washed as soon and as gently as possible. Scrub it with a soft brush under running water. Set it to dry in the sun or in a dry, warm room.

Long ago, ceremonies ritualized the special care of ginseng. Ancient hunters observed a spirit dwelling in the root, believing that it eluded all but the pure in heart. Cherokee Indians always passed by three ginseng plants before they gathered the fourth one they found. The Chinese ginseng hunter, once he found a plant, graced the spot with an altar and uttered thanks for such a gift. Each ritual reflected the sacredness of a single root discovered.

Today we praise the magic of ginseng, but we must not forget our part in preserving its magic. We need to recreate age-old ceremonies surrounding the plant, to keep it sacred. Perhaps, as our modern version of these respectful rituals, we should always replace some growing part of the ginseng we pick. Seeds, found red and ready to fall, can be tucked an inch into the soil. Auxiliary rootlets, often shooting off the main root of an elderly plant, can also be buried. The seed will take eighteen months to germinate, eight years to make a full-grown plant. The rootlet will make a full-grown plant more quickly. Either way, you will have repaid the forest in kind.

We must also learn to be frugal in our use of ginseng. A single root can last a person all winter long. Storage is no problem; dried roots stay potent for years. Once a day, chew a piece the size of a split pea. Remember the Tibetan monk who bites into a grain of rice one hundred times. Feel the root dissolve. It may seem bitter at first but it tastes sweet to initiates.

Or brew a cup of ginseng tea. Slice a full teaspoon of ginseng root into three cups of boiling water. Cover and let simmer twenty to thirty minutes. Pour this decoction over dried ginseng leaves, if you wish, and let it steep three minutes more. The Chinese prepare ginseng tea in silver dishes only, believing that more common metals sap the ginseng's powers.

Drink in that bitter, earthen taste; try to feel the effect this root has on you, quite apart from what history has made of it. Ginseng is subtle but sure. Steady small doses over a long period of time will affect you most noticeably. Chew a bit when you are tired, at the end of a hectic day. Chew a bit when you see a hectic day ahead. Ginseng will keep you clear-headed for the next event in your life.

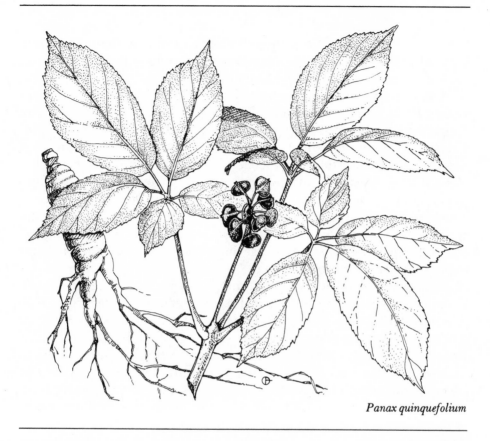

Panax quinquefolium

Those who chew ginseng for the first time ask, How can this root, whose effects are so undramatic, really make a difference? For a long time, science scoffed at ginseng along with other herbal remedies. The former government of China discouraged its use, but the present regime has re-introduced it into many hospitals. Scientists in Russia, China, and Japan began to take ginseng seriously almost thirty years ago, and in the last ten years Americans have joined their efforts. These scientists are discovering, miraculously, that many of the mythic claims for ginseng hold true.

Their experiments have followed two basic patterns. Some have analyzed the chemical composition of ginseng to discover active ingredients and understand how they affect the human body. Others have observed animals and humans who have ingested ginseng in controlled situations to see what effect the root has on their behavior. Both groups have made interesting discoveries.

The chemical investigators have found that, besides the many trace vitamins and minerals (vitamins A, B_1, B_2, C, and possibly E, calcium, magnesium, potassium, and others), ginseng contains its own "ginsenosides," active ingredients found exclusively in the plant. In small doses, ginsenosides stimulate the circulatory and nervous systems, but without the harmful side effects produced by caffeine or amphetamines. Chinese legends claim that ginseng produces a balance of energies. Current researchers agree, suggesting that it is an "adaptogen" capable of leveling off many of our internal systems. Ginseng will stimulate the mind and body when things are going smoothly; it calms the nerves when stress bears down.

Behavioral psychologists are coming up with similar results. They have put animals through abnormal stress situations to investigate how ginseng works. Rats subjected to extreme heat and cold survived longer with ginseng added to their food. Mice swam longer and faster when fed ginseng. Human subjects have proven ginseng's powers as well. Russian radio operators given ginseng felt less fatigue and decoded messages more accurately than usual. Elderly people have enjoyed increased initiative and pleasure in their work, increased stamina, and even increased muscle strength, given steady doses of ginseng.

Summing up years of research, Russian scientist N. Brekhman concluded that "ginseng preparations increase physical and mental efficiency, improve the accuracy of work, contribute to concentration, and prevent overfatigue." Other experimenters hope to prove ginseng effective in treating heart ailments, circulatory problems, diabetes, recovery after accidents or surgery, and even mental illness. Science is proving ginseng to be the miracle herb promised for centuries in myth.

But science can only go so far. It can name ingredients and observe effects, but it will never thoroughly penetrate the mystery of ginseng. Science will never explain how, amidst centuries of thoughtless exploitation, ginseng endures. Science can only give us more reasons to respect the mystery of ginseng.

Old Pomes

W E H A V E eaten pears and apples since the beginning. Their firm round shapes and brisk autumn flavors strike primeval chords within. Apple seeds nestled in prehistoric sites dating back some five thousand years. Human life as we know it, according to Judaeo-Christian myth, began with an apple. Eve ate the fruit and our troubles began. Cast out of Eden, Eve and her descendants had not only to plough and till; they had also to prune and graft, propagate and protect the pear and apple species. Now these plants count on human care.

The principles of pome propagation follow from the fact that apples and pears do not grow true to seed. A McIntosh tree will always bear McIntosh apples. But seedlings sprouting from those apples will not bear McIntosh fruit. The pollen of one apple variety fertilizes the blossom of another, so apple seeds sprout new breeds. When a choice fruit producer is discovered, orchardists take twigs from it and graft them to strong rootstock to make more trees. Leave the prize tree alone and its life will run its course, producing pomes for over a hundred years but eventually succumbing to old-age weariness and leaving no descendants to continue its line.

Wild pome trees will spring from seed, the fruits varying from tree to tree. Native crabapples grew on this continent before white settlers arrived. And even the cultivated varieties, brought over by European colonists, cast seeds that produced new stock. Most of the apple varieties we know today sprang from chance seedlings. A farmer tasted the unbidden fruit and, when it captured his fancy, he would tend and prune and propagate the tree so its pomes could be enjoyed by many. Even the ubiquitous Red Delicious apple can be traced back to one weedy upstart found outside an 1870s Iowa tree row.

Back then hundreds of varieties of apples made it to market. Now we can't find ten without a search. Even amidst such plenty, Thoreau bemoaned the loss of wild apples superseded by the cultivated kind. Today I mourn the passing of old-time apples in favor of a few bland varieties. Old-timers are the wild apples of our days. Aged trees still stand in abandoned orchards, their limbs half dead, bark peeling, overrun by vines. Winter Banana, Yellow Bellflower, Maiden Blush, Newtown Pippin—their names evoke images like the placards outside English country pubs. Sadly, some of these old-time varieties are lost forever. No one cared to cut budding twigs from the trees as they aged. Their fruits live on in memory only.

Those lucky enough to find old pome-bearing trees can contribute to their preservation. Untended pear and apple trees grow tall and shaggy, often falling victim to disease. Pruning helps. Saw off all dead limbs, cutting at an angle that lets rainwater run off rather than into the wound. Saw or clip off limbs and twigs that grow straight up or down or that head into the heart of the tree. Ideally pruning leaves a well-rounded crown growing from sturdy central limbs and trunk. Branches should spread so that the picker can climb and reach fruit easily. No branch should cross or touch another. Further care involves mowing and mulching the ground beneath the tree and keeping it clear of fallen fruits, which can house parasites or disease over winter. Care of old pome trees, year in, year out, may renew them.

Their fruits will inspire you to care even more, as you try a tart pear marmalade or my fall favorite, Hobo Chutney. Hobo Chutney makes the best of autumn's old pomes. I use Newtown Pippins (called Albemarle Pippins where I live) and Kieffer pears. Green turning golden red, both fruits suit the season. From the garden I gather tomatoes still green on the vine and onions plump from summer growing. From the woods I gather wild ginger roots as the leaves are turning under. I buy the raisins. I dice and mix roots and fruits in the following proportions: 3 apples, 3 pears, 3 green tomatoes, 1 onion, and a 2-inch length of wild ginger root. A quarter cup of raisins. Combine a quarter to a half cup of sweetening (sorghum, honey, or brown sugar) with a half cup of cider vinegar. Scatter in other herbs or spices: sassafras flakes, wild allspice berries, chopped cloves of wild garlic, powdered cinnamon, nutmeg, or cloves. Pour boiling sweet spiced vinegar over the fruits, then simmer until they are adequately

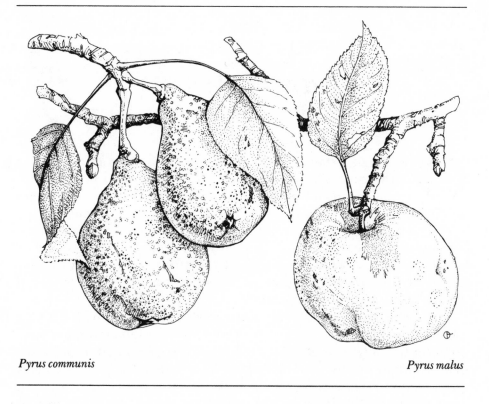

Pyrus communis   *Pyrus malus*

soft, half an hour or so. You can can the chutney or just refrigerate it in a covered jar. It makes a pleasing holiday gift, with the tang of wild roots and the character of old pears and apples.

Old pomes may not fruit picture perfect. Scabs and rust, worms and rot may have set into fruits or limbs. Nevertheless, we do our best to bring these trees more life. Some nurseries will help by joining old-time apple scions or cuttings onto vital rootstock, to keep old-timers growing. You send them cuttings; in two years they send you a two-year-old tree. In ten years you may take pleasure in tasting old pomes from a new tree. And, in the meantime, may you gather old pomes this autumn, blemished and misshapen as they may be. May you taste the special flavor of a Maiden Blush or a Newtown Pippin—full-bodied, sweet, insistent, divine.

Eating Acorns

Oak Trees stand, grand and aged, across this continent. Some of the same trees stood two hundred years ago, when spirits of nature haunted the oaks. Natives here and on other continents felt the presence of a god within the oak: a god which, through yearly cycles of shedding leaves and autumn fruits, stood tall and grew stronger every year. The god died grandly too, still reaching bleached and bare for years toward heaven. Beneath its rotting boughs, nuts scattered over centuries continue to set sprouts, grow leaves, and replenish the landscape with oak.

Humans and other animals have scrabbled for acorns for a long time. Gathering acorns during their mid-autumn falling doesn't seem to harm the new crop of oaks. We find so few compared to the many that oak trees produce. In those acorns we gather complete vegetable protein, up to six percent of their bulk. Acorns can sustain us. Acorns have sustained North American natives, European peasants, and they still sustain primitive peoples living today. Indians and colonists ate acorns from ancestors of the oak trees that now surround us.

Perhaps you were told in childhood, as I was, that acorns are poisonous. I was to keep them out of my mouth. And a nibble on the sly confirmed my mother's warning. The acorn tasted biting, bitter. Now I know that the unpleasant flavor of red oak acorns falling in my grandmother's Michigan backyard is typical of that variety, owing to the higher concentration of tannin in their nuts. If I had nibbled a white oak acorn instead, it might have tasted better (unless my mother's warning had served to make it too taste like poison)—because white oak acorns contain considerably less tannic acid than red. This fall I more knowingly nibbled white oak acorns raw. They tasted good, like raw chestnuts.

Look at an oak leaf's shape to determine whether the tree belongs to the group of red or white oaks. In red oak varieties, the major leaf

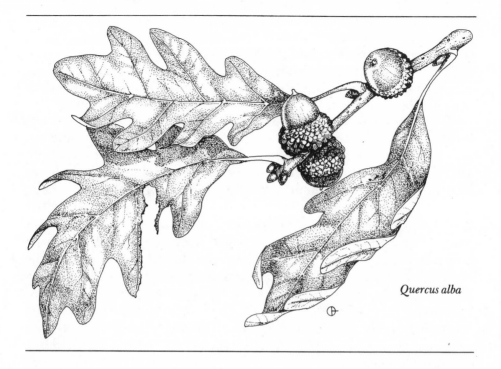

Quercus alba

veins terminate in points or spikes: black oaks, pin oaks, and blackjack oaks, for example. White oak leaves have rounded lobes instead: the white oaks, chestnut oaks, post oaks, bur oaks, for example. The inside of their acorn caps is smooth and the meat of their acorns tastes sweeter than that of the red oaks.

It's the tannin that makes acorns taste bitter. An acidic substance present in many plants, tannin has been gathered to treat leather and fix dyes. Its astringency makes all tannin-containing plants useful as medicinals. Oak bark, sassafras root bark, and sumac berries all brew healthful cleansing teas because of their astringent tannic acid content.

Tannin can be dissolved in water, and Indians devised methods for extracting the bitter principle. We can follow their practice, either by boiling the capped and shelled acorns or by letting them sit in a stream overnight. Flowing water will leach the tannic acid out. If you boil them, you will actually see the tannin coloring the water dark brown. You should change the water several times. Keep boiling the acorns, a quarter hour at a time, until the water stays light enough so that you can see the nuts through it after boiling. White oak acorns may take only half an hour's boiling. Red oak acorns may take more time than you're willing to spend.

Whether you leach or roast or grind first, it doesn't seem to matter. Indian recipes that remain with us call for every possible permutation of these three necessary procedures for preparing acorn meal. I find it easiest to leach the nuts in boiling water, roast them whole or quartered, then grind them in a grain mill. Acorns that have been boiled or soaked become soft enough to work with a mortar and pestle if you don't have a mill to grind them. You can also just chop soft acorns into fine pieces, adding cracked acorns to bread dough or muffin mixes. I've also roasted and ground the nuts, then leached the meal after grinding them, by tying it in a cheesecloth bag for boiling. Blenders and grain mills seem to work better with roasted acorns. Spread the nuts on a sheet and bake them in a slow oven, 250 to 300 degrees F. (120 to 150 degrees C.), for about an hour. As you experiment, you'll discover which acorn recipes fit your own kitchen habits and implements.

And you will discover your favorite ways to use acorn meal. Ground or chopped, it will enhance any recipe for bread, hot cakes, rolls, biscuits, or muffins. You can substitute the acorn meal for as much as half the flour required in a recipe. Or try some Acorn Muffins. Mix together 1½ cups flour, 1½ cups acorn meal or chips, 1 teaspoon salt, 3 teaspoons baking powder. Increase the flour if your acorns don't add up to this amount. Beat together ½ cup oil or melted butter, 2 eggs, ½ cup honey or sorghum molasses, and ½ cup buttermilk. Fold the wet briskly into the dry. Bake in greased muffin tins at 375 degrees F. (190 degrees C.) for 15 to 20 minutes. Brown and good.

Serving acorns, you are thanking not only the land, which gives us autumn nuts in plenty. You are also thanking the natives of this land, who gave of themselves to help us learn how to use the wilds of this continent. Those Indians live on in the few accounts we have of their lives, their wisdom, and their customs. May they live on in us as we recover the foods they ate, the herbs they gathered, and their belief in the spirit alive in the woods.

Wild Ginger

UTUMN pulls the life of plants underground. Leaves wilt and grow weary. They fall, creating a dense blanket to protect surviving parts below. Perennial roots bulge with dormant energy, stored until it is called up by the spring warmth. Following the turn of the seasons, we seek out roots in the fall: tawny chicory, potent ginseng, and pungent native wild ginger.

Several species of wild ginger hide in the cool, quiet shade of old mountain woods, both eastern and western ranges. From the Gaspé Peninsula clear west and south to the Arkansas Ozarks, from British Columbia down the coast into California, every rich forest must have its patches of wild ginger. Many a native American Indian tribe living amidst these forests gathered the fragrant root. They found wild ginger useful for digestion. They cooked with it and ate it to ease stomach pains. Indian women drank a strong tea of wild ginger root to prevent conception. When introduced to this North American native, colonists noted its distinct fragrance. They gave it a common name that reflects similarity in aroma, but not botanical fact. Tropical ginger (*Zingiber officinale*) grows fat, tuberous rootstocks and tall, leafy stems in steamy climates like Indonesia or Jamaica. Wild ginger (genus *Asarum*) grows crisp, slender rootstock under broad leaves in the shady forests of northern North America. Only their aroma relates the two plants.

That aroma is a sure mark of identification for the woodland wild ginger. Its leathery leaf, shaped like a wide, oval heart, stands no more than six or eight inches above the ground. An evergreen species (*Asarum arifolium*) supports a darker shiny leaf, marbled with white along the veins. Its deciduous counterpart (*Asarum canadense*) unfolds leaves a bit more hairy, unadorned green, wider and rounder. Beneath both leaf forms entwine shallow, sinewy, volatile roots. Disentangle some portion of the rootstock. Its fragrance stays on your fingers and lingers in the air. It invites further exploration.

Since one of wild ginger's biological effects is to ease too much gas in the digestive system—and also because it tastes delicious—I've taken to using the root as a seasoning whenever I cook beans. Here's a typical recipe for Spiced Black Beans. Soak 2½ cups of dried black beans overnight. The next day, toss in the following additions: a large chopped onion, a few minced cloves of wild garlic, a diced tomato, a 2-inch length of wild ginger, a teaspoon each of basil, dry mustard, nutritional yeast, salt, and cayenne pepper, 2 tablespoons each of honey or molasses and cider vinegar. Bring the pot to a boil and simmer for hours until the beans are soft and about to lose their skins. You will taste the wild ginger in a dish like this and you may feel its beneficent effects as well.

Wild ginger is not strictly interchangeable with Jamaica ginger. But experiment by using it, either fresh or dried, in some of your recipes. When I gather wild ginger, I leave hanging its numerous hairy tendrils. I scrub the roots with a soft brush and put them in a warm, dry place for a few days. The breadwarmer in a wood-burning cookstove is perfect. A very slow electric oven or the pilot light of a gas oven will also dry the roots gently. Outdoors, dry sunshiny days will work the best. Once the roots are brittle enough to snap, I store them in a covered jar. The hairs left hanging pulverize easily to substitute for tropical ginger powder.

The larger pieces remain for cooking beans or for pickling (see "Wild Spice") or for brewing hot teas through the winter. A strong cup of wild ginger tea makes an excellent pick-me-up, a naturally stimulating drink. (Remember that it was drunk by Indian women for contraceptive reasons. Use that information as you will: my research has provided no scientific confirmation of the practice.) For each cup of water add three two-inch lengths of dried wild ginger root. Bring the pot to a boil, cover and bubble gently for half an hour, as you would brew any other tea made from roots. A thick, spicy aroma will fill the air. That aroma—it evokes images. I sense seekers after exotic spices and native Americans gathering autumn roots. In that aroma I can almost feel the dark deep woods as winter hovers.

Asarum arifolium

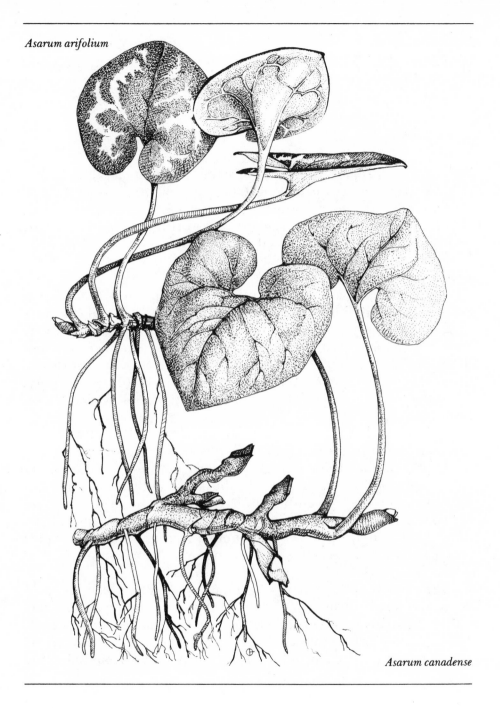

Asarum canadense

Nutting

M O S T people recognize a nut when they see it fall, although not that many go out looking. Our continent provides several wild nut varieties, particularly in areas east of the great plains. Walnuts and hickory nuts make a search worthwhile. Go out looking with a satchel or—as it happened to me this fall—you will come upon bushels of nuts with nothing but the shirt on your back to carry them home in.

Our native black walnut is related in shape and taste to the commercially grown English or Carpathian walnut. Yet, while the husk of the English walnut slips right off, leaving an easily crackable woody shell, the black walnut presents more of a problem. The wild nut develops a thick green fleshy husk. When time comes ripe, the leaves drop and one sees round nuts clustered along stark, straight branches. Then the nuts drop too, falling green and turning black as the husk begins to decompose.

To harvest black walnuts, one must remove shelled nut from husk, then extract nut meats from nut shell. It is a tedious process but it can be simplified. Euell Gibbons suggests wearing gloves and heavy boots and simply toeing nuts out of the husks as one finds them. But sometimes one finds green husks still clinging to the shell, and these are not easily coaxed away. A lot of people I know remove husks in an unromantic but effective way. We dump a load of unhusked walnuts on the driveway. A few days of traveling over them with one or two automobiles works the husks right off the shells.

The next problem is cracking them open. Black walnuts grow dense and woody shells with meats interwoven into baroque chambers within. Again my practice is indelicate: I take a hammer, I take a rock, I place the nut on the rock and smash it. Well—*smash* may not be the word, since a proper tap will crack the nut without demolishing the

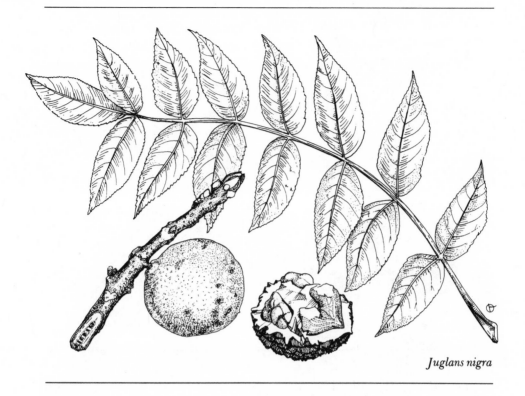

Juglans nigra

meat inside. Try hammering them inside a large cardboard carton. It's easier to clean up and it will catch the little pieces.

Once you have cracked open enough walnuts to fill a cup or two, you can make Black Walnut Ice Cream. Heat in a small saucepan ½ cup sorghum molasses or maple syrup and 1½ cups sugar. Bring to a bubble and blend your nut meats into these ingredients. As you add them, take one last look to be sure you haven't left chips of shell among the meats. Once this concoction cools, add to it 2 quarts milk, 2 beaten eggs, and ¼ cup cream. Add a pinch of salt, put it in the ice cream maker, and start cranking.

Hickory nuts come out of their shells a little more easily than walnuts. Their husks split neatly but their shells take a hammer too. At least ten varieties of wild hickory trees grow on our continent. Often hickories dominate a forest where they're found. Not all hickory nuts

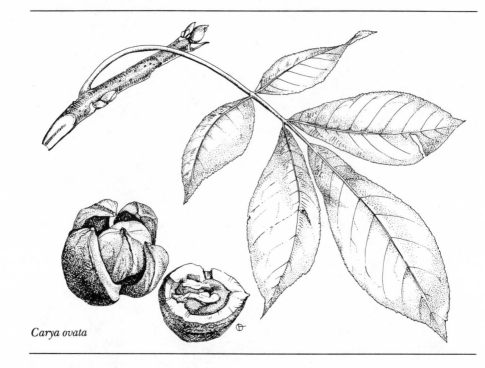

Carya ovata

are appetizing, though. The shagbark hickory is always sweet, though not always substantial. Look for long, shaggy flakes of bark curving off a good-sized tree, and look too for half-inch-thick nut husks that fall off in quarters. Other hickory varieties show husks that are thinner and need peeling. Beware, for among those varieties is the bitternut hickory, which looks like any other tasty nut but has that same unpleasant taste of tannin found in the red oak acorn. I learned from one bitter experience to distinguish varieties of hickory nuts as I gather them. Nothing like sprinkling hickories over a dish of ice cream and getting a mouthful of bitternut.

Our eastern forests used to provide yet another outstanding nut: the American chestnut. Remains of those grand old trees still haunt the woods in Virginia. Gray striated logs decompose slowly on the woodland floor. Stumps with three-foot diameters stand, moss-covered and weathered yet still remarkably sturdy, considering they were left behind about fifty years ago. The chestnut trees were first attacked by the lumber trade, since the gray wood built up strong and lasted longer than just about any other kind. And then the blight hit—a fungus called *Endothia parasitica*. It entered the chestnut population in the thirties and killed off all but perhaps fifty aged American chestnut trees still standing across the continent.

Nowadays some forests abound in little chestnut seedlings. With their long, slim, scalloped leaves, they grow to be twelve or thirteen years old and may even produce nuts one year; then they succumb to the blight. But curiously, Italian botanists report that their chestnut trees, also endangered, are making a comeback. A virus, a natural combatant of the chestnut blight, has entered the trees and is reviving the European chestnut population. American researchers are actively seeking an interchange of seedlings and virus cultures, hoping that this generation of American chestnuts can be saved as well.

The woods must have looked very different when the chestnuts stood tall. And autumn nutting would have been different too. If scientists can find a way to save the chestnuts, so that today's seedlings can grow into trees, our forests may regain the grandeur of yesteryear. But, for the time being, we search forests for walnuts and hickory nuts, only occasionally finding the traces of a chestnut civilization now past.

WINTER

Sunflower Potatoes

WHEN I first moved to a country home in Virginia—it was in the fall—I remember discovering bright yellow flowers blooming atop tall stalks at the edge of a neighbor's cornfield. The leaves were rough and hairy. The stalks stood taller than I did. The flowers shone brightly and, to my delight, kept their color in a vase on our kitchen table for nearly a month.

Little did I know then that beneath these cheerful flowers were growing the thick, knotty tubers that are among the most widely favored wild edibles gathered in the United States and Canada. Jerusalem artichokes, many people call them. "Sunchokes" is one of their commercial names. Their botanical name, *Helianthus tuberosus,* accurately describes them as tuberous relations to the common garden sunflower. I like to call them sunflower potatoes, and now that I know what to look for, I see them blooming everywhere.

They flower in early to mid-autumn, and that is the best time to scout them out. Other sunflowers bloom similarly, with bright yellow-petaled, yellow-centered daisy-like blooms atop strong, hairy stalks. I look first at the stalk: sunflower potato stalks are round, although furry, while many of their counterparts have vertical ribbing running up the stem. But if I have any doubt I pull up a single stalk. The roots will tell the story. Only the sunflower potato grows a thick, substantial, tuberous root.

As with any other root crop, sunflower potato tubers should not be gathered while the plants flower. Only after frost hits the plant tops, sending their vitality back underground, do the roots attain their

Helianthus tuberosus

sweetest, most nutritious form. Identify sunflower potatoes as they bloom and mark the spot. Then return when blooms are gone, and return all winter long. Gather only as many as you can use in the next day or so, and leave the rest underground. They spoil in the refrigerator, but they keep fresh under the soil. Not all that many wild things favor winter gathering—a plus for sunflower potatoes in my book.

Those who live in colder climates, where the freeze line sinks beneath the six-to-ten-inch depth of sunflower potato tubers, might consider mulching a patch of the plants when they find them. Cover it with four to six inches of hay, newspaper, or grass clippings in the fall, and you will discourage the ground around them from freezing. While freezing does not hurt the tubers, it is hard to get a shovel through dirt frozen solid. You can more easily lift up the mulch throughout the winter, whenever you want to harvest the crop.

Sunflower potatoes contribute nutrients as well as variety to any wintertime meal. High in vitamins and minerals, especially thiamine and potassium, they are a valuable fresh vegetable when few others remain in the garden or greengrocer's. Although they taste sweet and feel starchy—kind of a cross between an apple and a potato—they are extremely low in calories. Sunflower potatoes contain inulin, a carbohydrate more complex than glucose or sucrose and safer in a diabetic diet.

And sunflower potatoes taste good. Personally, I prefer them raw to cooked. The flavor released by cooking is quite different from the flavor of a crisp, cold slice of raw tuber. The simplest way to enjoy the roots is to scrub and slice them for a plate of raw munchies, as hors d'oeuvres, a side salad, or a snack. But don't resist experimenting with cooked sunflower potatoes either. Many simple recipes call for the roots to be boiled or baked for a cooked vegetable. I prefer to make a soup of them.

Cover about 4 cups of sliced, scrubbed sunflower potatoes with 2 or 3 quarts of water. Boil them gently until soft, about 30 to 40 minutes, while you prepare the rest of the soup. Soften a large onion, sliced thin, and ample wild garlic in 2 tablespoons of oil. Add a touch of your favorite seasoning—I like to use sage, basil, and a smidgen of curry powder. Once the onions and garlic are soft, you can also add shredded greens—kale or spinach from the garden, wintercress gathered and cooked once, chickweed fresh. Soften the greens in the oil as well. Keep a lid on. Once the sunflower potatoes are soft, mix everything together. Taste and see what it needs—a dash of salt or soy, a pinch of nutritional yeast might give it some zest. I find that this soup improves dramatically overnight, so I try to make it the day before I want to eat it.

Once you find the sunflower potatoes growing near you (and no doubt you will, since they grow across the continent), you can start experimenting. Many like a sunflower potato salad, made by blanching and dicing the tubers, tossing them in with other salad ingredients and a flavorful dressing. Others use sunflower potatoes in a vegetable casserole, although I'll warn you that their distinctive flavor will often overpower the more subtle vegetables in your dish. That's why I usually keep them raw and separate, so I can enjoy their flavor on its own.

An additional beauty of sunflower potatoes is their never-ending will to live. As you scrub and trim the roots you have gathered, save any scraps. As long as they have a single eye on them, they are viable plant starters. With each trimming, plant the scraps in your newly formed sunflower potato patch. Find a good sunny spot on your lawn or near your garden, where you don't mind plants reaching ten feet tall and spreading roots further year by year. My friend Erbin (who is to sunflower potatoes what Johnny Appleseed was to apples) advises friends to plant a sunflower potato patch on the south side of the house, for summer shade and warmer winter harvests. Once you start your patch, you won't have to go out looking for the plants. They will grow like wild in your own backyard, this year, next year, and every year thereafter.

Winter Greens

THE FOREST floor is caked with dead leaves. It's the end of autumn, coming into the cold. Thin slips of chickweed brave the freeze. Pastures, orchards, even front yard stoops and city lots fill in with chickweed once summer growth retreats. Bright green tendrils grow long and low, watery and delicate. Small heart-shaped

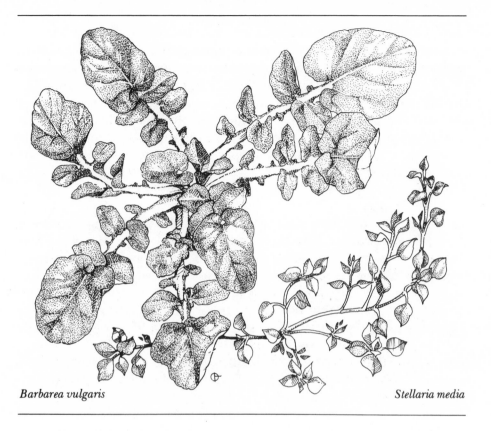

Barbarea vulgaris   *Stellaria media*

leaves branch opposite one another from a thin stem. Leaves cluster in
a cheery rosette at the stem's growing end. As summer approaches,
chickweed fades beyond its flower. Checkweed is a winter find.

So is wintercress, earlier mentioned as wild broccoli (in "Wild
Garden Before the Plough"). Tougher leaves, deeper green than
chickweed, spring from a growing center, making a foliated bouquet
wherever the land is cleared and warm enough to support a bit of life.
Creesy greens, as they are called by country folk who gather them
around here in Virginia, often appear in supermarkets by the pound;
they taste so good and grow so abundantly in early winter and in early
spring.

Wintercress thrives in pastures and on roadsides throughout the
northeastern states and Canada, and southwest toward Texas. It can be

found in certain select areas of the plains and the northwest coast as well, according to the U.S. Department of Agriculture. Maybe someone once planted it there. The USDA calls chickweed a "cosmopolitan weed" because it thrives across this continent and several others, in "dooryards, lawns, waste places, cultivated areas, woodlands, thickets, and meadows"—in other words, just about anywhere. But the USDA looks upon chickweed as a pest: "especially bad," their literature reads, "in gardens, alfalfa, strawberry beds, and nurseries." In their eyes, chickweed is a nuisance. To mine, chickweed looks fine.

Settlers may have brought both wintercress and chickweed with them, or they may have found the familiar plants growing here when they came. Certainly they and natives who knew the plants knew of their uses too. They probably knew to cook wintercress, as does anyone who tries a taste of all but the tenderest of new-grown leaves. Raw wintercress leaves harbor bitterness, but cooking sweetens them. One often cooks wintercress like poke, in two waters, throwing out the bitterness with the first water, using it to feed a window-ledge plant. And as for chickweed, settlers must have known (as I knew from the first nibble) that it tastes best as fresh raw greens, growing nutrients in a time of winter dearth. Chickweed can be cooked, but why cook it? It tastes so good and provides such food value when one eats it raw.

I always chew a little chickweed when I find it, to get that burst of vitamins A and C, sunshine for my journey. It adds bright green to salads and sandwiches and ornaments beautiful canapés. Try chickweed chopped into slaw; it adds color and flavor. But if you would prefer winter greens to cook with, find wintercress instead. Remember to take your knife, so you can cut each plant off a little beneath ground level. That way you will gather the sweet white inner core as well as the leaves.

I like to make Wild Greens and Garlic Soup. Scrub and dice five potatoes, cover with water, and boil thirty minutes while you prepare the rest of the soup. Wash and trim about two cups of wintercress greens and half a cup of wild garlic bulbs or chives or both. Cover with a quart of boiling water and boil gently about four minutes. Pour off the water. Into three tablespoons of oil in a frying pan toss a teaspoon of your favorite cooking herbs. When they begin to sizzle, add the wild garlic and greens. Stir and simmer for ten minutes, then add to the potato broth. You may want to season the soup or thicken it with milk or grated cheese or a white sauce. But give the simple recipe a sip before you do.

Winter greens give me something to look forward to with cold weather coming on. Both of these taste good and healthy; both grow abundantly. And both show up just when you need them, as northern winds begin to blow and garden greens are long gone. I don't consider chickweed or wintercress pests; they are blessings in weedy disguise.

Rose Hips

ONE SEES in many wild flowers the promise of wild fruit. Early strawberry flowers bloom underfoot, then rubus branches blossom out in white. Apple and pear blooms bespeckle the spring horizon. Spring froth summons autumn harvest. We mark the flowers, waiting for fruit. Then comes summer, and roses bloom. A rose is a rose, and we cherish it for its flower. Too many of us ignore its fruit. Blooming roses promise rose hips, the delicate, sweet, potent fruit of the rose.

Not all roses have hips. But those that do form fruit, like their relative the apple, behind the bloom. The fragrant petals fall, leaving a burnt brown calyx attached to the base of a fruit that bulges, green and growing, through the summer. Winter cold brings out reds as glowing as the color of the flower itself. Red rose hips are ripe. They detach easily from the stalk, and many feel as fleshy as any other fruit. You can even take a bite out of the bigger rose hips, just as if they were little apples. Ignoring the seeds, you'll taste the sweet acid flavor of the fruit of the rose.

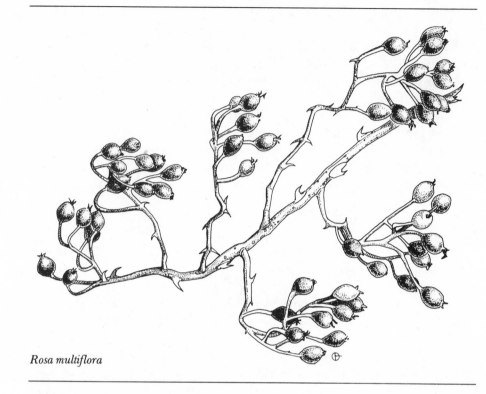

Rosa multiflora

The acid you taste is ascorbic: vitamin C. Rose hips provide as much vitamin C as just about any fruit you could name, including the citrus that we commonly hail as the sunshine fruit. Euell Gibbons provided us some figures that are astounding: a cup of rose hip pulp provides vitamin C equivalent to that of more than a hundred oranges. Now it would take a lot of rose hips to make a cup of puree, but one can look at the figures another way. With every tablespoon of rose hips you include in your winter pot of tea, you add the equivalent of five or six large oranges. Not bad for an inconspicuous garden treasure.

In England, where roses bloom with abandon, I've seen hips as big as apricots, hips the color of red burgundy, and long thin hips, more than an inch in length, bright orange as the setting sun—all growing in the same garden at Sissinghurst. Over here, I've come across equally beautiful rose hips, although it has taken a bit more looking. In my

Virginia neighborhood many farms are bordered with hedges of the multiflora rose. These abundantly offer small white blooms in early summer, festive and fragrant enough to create a potpourri around them (see "Essence of Spring"). Now, as winter surrounds us, those hedgerows are polkadotted with crimson bounty. The hips are small and not too fleshy, but their numbers make up for their size.

Whether you find one rosebush or a whole row of them, gathering rose hips is worth your while. I usually dry them as soon as I find them, trimming off stems and leafy parts and placing them in the oven warmer (a low electric oven setting or the gas stove pilot light works fine) for about an hour. As with so many other wild things, rose hips have moisture that can deceive. If they are not adequately dried before storing, they will mold. Cap your jar of dried rose hips and leave it on a sunny windowsill for an afternoon. If moisture collects, they need more drying.

I like to keep dried rose hips on hand to add to teas throughout the winter. I even drop a few into a pot of English breakfast tea: they brighten the color, sweeten the flavor, and add vitamin value to a morning brew. Rose hip tea is flavorful on its own as well. Using a rounded tablespoon of dried hips per cup, crush them slightly and pour boiling water on to steep. Orangy-red riches will sift through your teacup, the color of good health through the coming year.

Rose hip syrups and jellies can be a special treat, although they require some preparation. You may use fresh or dried hips. Add half a cup of water per cup of hips (somewhat less if you use fresh fruit) and simmer until the skins burst and the pulp floats free. In most cases, you'll want to strain this potion through several thicknesses of cheesecloth to extract the seeds. Some recipes suggest that you strain the hips, then simmer the seeds in water once again so as to get all of their sweet nectar before you discard them. Now you have a thin, rosy puree that can be used in a basic jelly recipe. Add not quite the equivalent amount of sugar or half as much honey, boil, add packaged pectin, boil again, and spoon into jars. The color will be your roses' variation on red. One warning: vitamin C decomposes rapidly, so rose hip jelly should be prepared with a minimum of boiling and standing.

Starting with the same puree, you can also make a light Rose Hip

Custard, a bland dessert that belongs in an English tea garden. Blend together 1½ cups milk, ⅓ cup honey or sorghum molasses, 1 cup rose hip puree, and ⅛ teaspoon salt. Beat 4 whole eggs. Add them to the rose hip mixture, then beat again. Pour into custard cups. Set the cups in a pan of hot water and bake them for about an hour in a slow oven, about 300 degrees F. (150 degrees C.). The color and flavor are as delicate as the roses from which the recipe began.

Once you find rose hips, you'll find ways to use them. If you've been growing garden roses, you may be growing rose hips too. The most particular of rose gardeners snip off the bloom when it withers. But they are snipping off the promise of rose fruiting too. A rose isn't just a rose: it is a flower announcing fruit yet to come. Let roses go, and you can bring in baskets of rose hips come winter, a cold-weather bouquet.

Winter Sprouts

M O S T weeds don't make it through winter. They need warm rain and steady sun. Frozen soil inhibits root growth; snow-falls discourage sprouts. Even a plant like watercress, which usually positions itself in flowing water, gets burned by a freeze. If you live in an area where snows fall over several months, you know that small sigh of sadness when you go out to gather wild things and frost has taken over.

This year I've been cultivating weeds indoors to ease those winter doldrums. I've got chicory, dandelion, and poke roots potted in buckets in a kitchen corner. I've got watercress stretching out of a pot standing in fresh water. And I've got chickweed gaily going to seed three months early on the windowsill. While my wild winter garden doesn't provide the abundance of the outdoors, it grows leaves enough to garnish winter meals with sprigs of wild flavor, nutrients, and color.

The classic cellar garden is patterned after the greeneries of the chefs of France. By giving hardy perennial roots a warm, dark place and plenty of water, we can grow blanched greens. In the last lingering days of autumn, identify good-sized plants of dandelion and chicory. They will have passed their prime: dandelion's just a leafy cluster, chicory's a dried flower stalk. Young leaves may have emerged in the sun of Indian summer. Were it not for the coming freeze, these plants would go on forever. We help them to achieve everlasting green.

A large juice can will hold one plant; three- to five-gallon buckets give room for the lengthy roots of several. If you use clay pots, you have to water daily. Cans or plastic buckets hold the moisture in. Dirt gathered from the outside should probably be sterilized by baking twenty minutes at 200 degrees F. (95 degrees C.) or pouring boiling water through it. Set your shovel in deep; try to get most of the deep-reaching taproots. Set them down into warm potted earth. Sprinkle with warm water. See that the soil settles in around the roots. Set your weed pots in a warm, dark spot, in the cellar or under a carton in an obscure corner of the house. Make sure that the soil stays moist but not waterlogged. Give your plants warmth and water. Growth begins to stir. In three to six weeks, bleached potherbs emerge, white for lack of light, mild in flavor, and tender to taste.

I've found that a weed garden will also grow on the windowsill, providing green potherbs too. Out of curiosity, I potted a thick patch of chickweed this winter. That was before heavy frosts hit the leaves outdoors, clearing the way for ice and snow to cover. No chickweed has stirred outdoors for more than a month now, but on the windowsill my plant is trying to flower. I potted it and treat it like a houseplant, watering it when dry. I clip off maturing sprigs and toss them over salads. The taste is true, the color deep. This chickweed provides us vitamins when we most need them: when we can't gather them outside.

Same goes for my windowsill watercress. While snow covers the earth, our spring still flows, supporting sprigs of cress that don't dare raise their leaves above water level. If the stream freezes over, though, the plant dives under till spring. But, before that happens, watercress is easily uprooted and potted. Its only special need is constant water to the roots. So I set the plants in a dirt-filled flowerpot in a bowl of water, which I fill fresh every day. The little cress plants are stretching out, enjoying the sunshine as if they were on winter vacation.

Other weeds take well to indoor adaptation. Mints thrive inside. Wild onions in a pot replace chives. Perhaps even violets or sheep sorrel would respond to potting—but I'll have to wait until next winter to find out. The ground is ice-hard. Nature's roots hide in icy hibernation, while inside, a few weeds still thrive on warmth and human kindness.

Persimmons

WITHIN the woody network of vegetation stretching across the winter sky, persimmon branches stand out, still dotted with orange fruit into the coldest months. Small and shapely, with chunky bark a charcoal black, the persimmon tree is often found standing solitary at the edge of a pasture. Alone, it branches out fully, but in crowded woods, its fruited limbs climb high, straight up to the sun. The fruits cling close to twigs and branches, some the diameter of a quarter, others bulging large as plums on a healthy tree. Persimmons range through the southeastern third of the nation: from New York across to Arkansas, south to Florida and Texas. Country neighbors can tell you if they grow nearby.

Looking up, you may see the plump fruits silhouetted against the sky. Or, if you cast your glance earthward, fallen persimmons may signal a tree above. Many of the persimmons will hang too high to

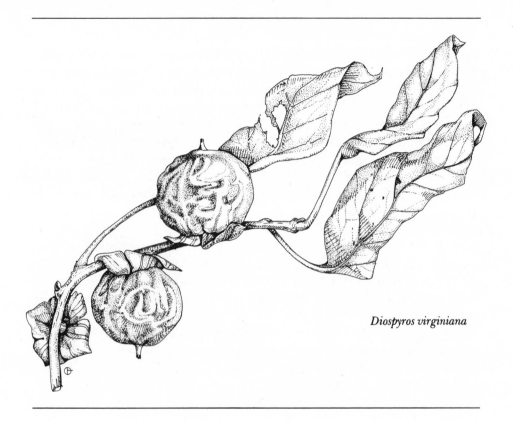

Diospyros virginiana

reach. To gather a treeful, I often spread a large sheet or tarpaulin around the trunk. I grab hold of the tree and shake long and hard. Orange nuggets come tumbling down. But be warned: they often smash on landing. Ask friends to lift the sheet off the ground to catch them more gently. As long as they don't collect dirt, though, smashed persimmons are as good as whole.

Before the frost, persimmons are tough, sour, and distasteful. Once winter strikes, the skins wither and the flesh softens. Freezing weather changes the taste and texture of the persimmon to a gooey treat.

The seeds and stems of persimmons must be extracted from the pulp before it can be used in cooking. A food mill is ideal for the purpose. Second best, mash the fruit through a sieve or colander with a wooden spoon. You can just pick out the pits with your fingers, but that can get messy.

Whichever way you choose to separate fruit from seeds, the result will be a sweet, sticky bowl of persimmon pulp with a tempting smell, a radiant color, and special flavor to add to holiday sweets. I like to give Sugar Plum Fruit Cakes to friends as gifts. Melt a package of powdered yeast in ⅛ cup lukewarm water or juice. Stir into it ¼ cup honey, ¼ cup buttermilk, a beaten egg, and a cup of persimmon pulp. Add the following solid ingredients: 1½ cups whole grain flour, ½ cup corn-meal, ¼ teaspoon salt, and ½ cup powdered milk. You may also add your choice of fruits and nuts—walnuts, hickory nuts, pecans, figs or dates, currants or raisins, grated coconut, diced apple sprinkled with lemon juice. Also add a little spice. Mix everything together well. You may let the batter rise half an hour for extra lightness or put it in the oven right away. Bake it for 45 to 55 minutes at 350 degrees F. (175 degrees C.).

Sometimes, even when persimmons look and smell sticky-sweet, the fruit will have slight green aftertaste that seems to stick to teeth and gums. Don't be discouraged: the bad taste will disappear in the cooking. Try Persimmon Waffles for a warm winter-morning break-fast. Mix together 2 cups flour, 3 teaspoons baking powder, and ½ teaspoon salt. Beat the yolks of 3 eggs; add to them 1 tablespoon honey or sorghum molasses, 1 cup persimmon pulp, ¼ cup sweet milk or buttermilk, ¼ cup water, and ½ cup oil or melted butter. Blend all together swiftly. Beat the 3 egg whites until stiff and fold them into the batter. After spooning the batter onto the griddle, try sprinkling it with coconut, sesame or sunflower seeds, wheat germ, chopped nuts, or raisins before closing the lid. Add a little bit more liquid if you'd rather make pancakes with persimmons.

All winter long I use persimmon pulp as a fruity addition to any sweet bread or cake recipe, using just that much less liquid and reducing the sweetening somewhat. Often I can or freeze the pulp so I can enjoy persimmons spring, summer, and fall too. You can substitute persimmons for bananas in bread or for applesauce in cake. Wrap up a Sugar Plum Fruit Cake for a home-gathered, home-cooked holiday gift. Visions of sugar plums will dance in the dreams of some children this Christmas, but others will taste the real thing.

Wild Holidays

THANK goodness for holidays to cheer us through the cold. And thank goodness for wild evergreens to ornament the way. Holiday boughs seem all the more festive when gathered in the wild. Each Christmas spray reflects the growing year. Under summer sun leaves thrived and berries ripened. I come now, under a winter sun cold and shiny, gathering wild evergreens and gay red berries to decorate home for the holidays.

Most regions have their resident evergreens. They stand, full and blue against the cool gray trunks of naked deciduous trees. Pines, cedars, and spruces: each tree offers a distinctive pattern of needles, branches, and cones, traditional wreathing materials. Southern regions offer broadleaf evergreens too: magnolias, holly, rhododendron.

Mountain laurel is my favorite Christmas evergreen. It can be gathered throughout the eastern mountain regions of this continent. Though harmful to farm animals that might happen upon it (and also to humans, were they to taste the unappetizing leaves), mountain laurel's looks appeal. Its snarled, striated shrub-trunks open into bouquets of glossy evergreen. In spring, clusters of pink and white flowers bedeck those bouquets. You'll know you're in a mountain laurel thicket when you have to stoop to pass under overhanging boughs. These are magical places, shaped for elves and gnomes rather than for people.

Once I've snipped a green bouquet of mountain laurel, I gather other wild things for shape and color. Sumac berry clusters add their velvet red to holiday drapings. Dried milkweed pods accent the arrangement with a white arabesque. Dried weedflowers—yarrow, self-heal, goldenrod, so many others—still offer graceful forms if not fragrance. The simplest dried grasses lend lines to a winter bouquet. Let your imagination and the world outside carry you beyond tradition as you create wild holiday festoons.

You might try using flexible honeysuckle or grape vines to form a

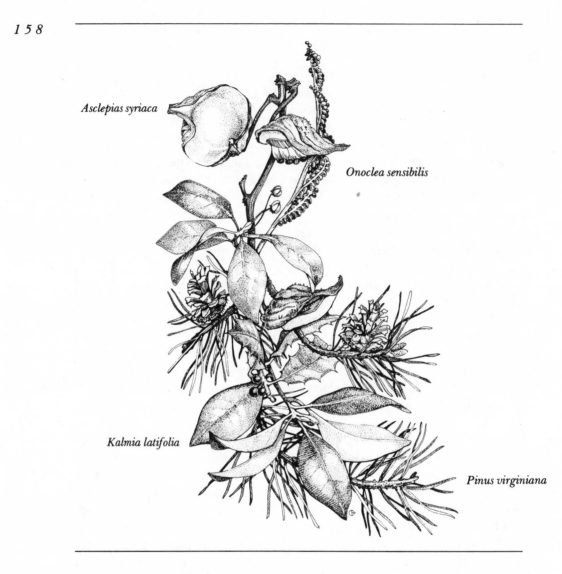

Asclepias syriaca

Onoclea sensibilis

Kalmia latifolia

Pinus virginiana

base for a wild wreath. Begin with a single vine, one-quarter to one-half inch in width, in length about four times the diameter of the wreath you envision. Twist the vine upon itself four times over, letting its kinks entangle with one another, binding into a circle. Then weave additional viny strands in and out and around that circle until you have a tight mat of interwoven vines. The tendrils that still hang can be used to lash over the greens, berry stalks, and dried flowers you poke into this home-fashioned frame.

Although most green life is fallen and snow-buried, winter wild things still abound with which to decorate a home in the holiday spirit. Berries and flowers remind us of summer's bounty, while evergreens remind us that nature lives on through the cold. We bring in sprigs of red and green and golden, hung in corners and arranged on the mantelpiece. Wild winter bouquets speak a warm welcome to friends and family, acknowledging ties that bind us closer with each turning of another year.

Periwinkle

PERIWINKLE is more than just a pretty ground cover. It has an interesting past and a promising future. Legends about periwinkle date back further than the facts we have about it, portraying a plant with influence over the devil. Herbalists proclaimed its powers. Apuleius, Roman author from the second century A.D., described periwinkle's powers thus: "This wort is of good advantage for many purposes, that is to say, first against devil sickness and demoniacal possessions and against snakes and wild beasts and against poisons and for various wishes and for envy and for terror and that thou mayst have grace, and if thou hast the wort with thee thou shalt be prosperous and ever acceptable." (Translation from Maud Grieve's *Modern Herbal*, Dover, 1971.) Modern advertising could not give the plant a better promotion.

And modern science has discovered more reasons to revere the periwinkle plant. Certain components of the Madagascar species, crimson-flowered *Vinca rosea*, inhibit cell growth. Doctors now include in cancer chemotherapy treatments steady doses of vinblastine sulfate or vincristine sulfate, two alkaloids extracted from the tropical periwinkle plant. While the vinca alkaloids sometimes produce unpleasant side effects, they effectively slow down tumorous cell reproduction. Periwinkle is no home cure for cancer, but these vinca extracts are among the most promising treatments for cancer today.

The periwinkle that grows, wild or cultivated, around the United States and Canada is a smaller and less potent relative of the Madagascar breed. Its local appearance only reminds us of the worldwide search for cancer treatments deriving from the plant world. *Vinca minor* covers wooded corners, orchard spots, and landscaped yards with its shiny evergreen leaves. Its appearance in the wild often means the land was earlier inhabited. Early blue flowers spin open in the spring. Hybrids bloom pink or white or purple. Closely related, *Vinca major* stands higher, grows larger leaves and flowers, and doesn't take so kindly to the wild. You will never discover a Madagascar periwinkle growing in the United States or Canada, outside a greenhouse. But the periwinkles you will find here have their own practical uses.

Periwinkle is a strong astringent, contracting tissue and reducing secretions. Modern herbalists prescribe it for many internal bleeding disorders, particularly excessive menstrual flow and hemorrhoids. This same astringent property explains the old-time periwinkle cure for a bleeding nose: bruise a leaf and stick it up your nostril. The astringency acts as a hemostat, drying up what ails you. Folks prescribe periwinkle leaf for toothache and bleeding gums too.

Periwinkle is also an herbal sedative. Folk traditions prescribe it for nightmares, hysteria, and fits. Maybe here is where the tales of influencing devils began. Able to calm the soul and assure one of deep sleeping, periwinkle drives away the demons of a troubled night. It is one of the herbs, along with pennyroyal and strawberry leaves, that I put into my minstrel tea. Doubtless this calming quality contributes to the effects of my home-brewed tea on mind and body during stressful days. To brew a cup of periwinkle tea, crush about twenty leaves into a pot and pour over them one cup of boiling water. Periwinkle tea tastes herby and bitter, but once inside, it soothes.

Since periwinkle is evergreen, you need not gather it one season for another. Indeed periwinkle, like wintergreen, would lose its potency if

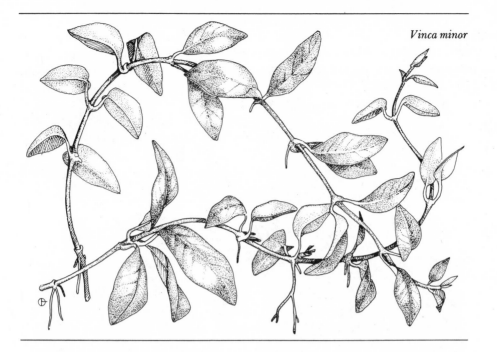

Vinca minor

dried like many a summertime herb. So, if you find periwinkle on an outing away from home, you're better off gathering a living plant to set into the ground, rather than gathering leaves to dry and store. Periwinkle transplants easily, doesn't mind poor soil, and doesn't need a lot of sunlight.

The best time to transplant periwinkle would be in early spring or early fall. Taking a few rooted shoots from a healthy clump, whether in the wild or your friend's backdoor garden, you actually help by thinning out the patch and giving remaining plants a place to grow. Dig down three inches, to get beneath the shallow roots. Try to take a clump of dirt with them. Since periwinkle doesn't mind poor soil or shady corners, it has become a successful nursery item and can be readily purchased at greenhouses if none turns up wild.

Whether you buy it or gather it, periwinkle should soon begin to fill the open spaces in your world. It spreads like wild. Those flowers, pale but seeming bright, among the first harbingers of springtime, will cheer you every year. The leaves, waxy green all winter long, will heal and soothe you. And, while this little periwinkle may not cure cancer, it will remind you of the international network of research now going on, inspired in part by the effectiveness of periwinkle extracts, to find other wild plants successful in treating human ills.

Praying Mantis Egg Case

EVERY summer garden should have a resident praying mantis. Winter is the time to find yours.

   This large, slender insect moves deliberately through the vegetables, bright green as the newest leaf. Its head swivels sharply, peering at anything that moves. It strikes at prey with precision, singling out some of the most troublesome garden pests as its targets.

   The mantid's body is designed for carnivorous habits. Its back two pairs of legs are long and spindly, for cautious stalking through leaves and twigs. Its front pair of legs, strong and fleshy, extend again the length of its body. Needle-sharp barbs line the segments of leg that do the grabbing. Once the mantid captures its prey, it holds on tight.

   Whoever named this insect saw those treacherous legs in another light. At rest, the mantis folds its spiked front legs up under its chin. The solemn, motionless stance it then assumes earned it the name praying mantis (the scientific name: *Mantis religiosa*). No scientist has discovered the deity worshiped by these creatures, but their sacrificial rites are fully documented. Grasshoppers, beetles, caterpillars: instead of finding them nibbling at garden vegetables, you will find them being devoured by this roving beast.

   Now, in the dead of winter, the mantis population is dormant. Last summer's insects left behind egg cases in fields and thickets. To

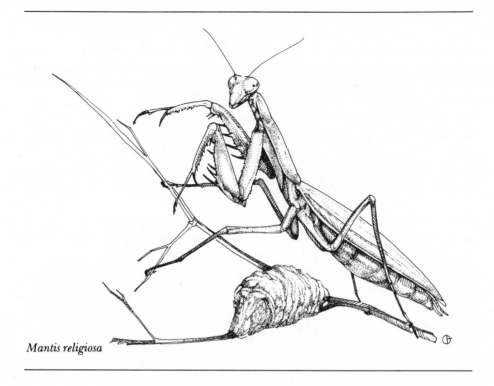

Mantis religiosa

produce these egg cases, the praying mantis danced a haunting mating ritual. The male insect, smaller and sleeker than his partner, will approach to fertilize her. As they unite, the female becomes ravenous for protein to fortify her for the coming task of laying eggs. For lack of other food, she may turn on her partner. As he performs his male duties, she devours him.

The female mantis then begins her solitary dance, abdomen slowly undulating with fertilized eggs. She secretes a foamy substance in which she implants her brood. Then she departs, weakened by her efforts, leaving behind a tough, brown, nut-sized egg case suspended on a limb or branching weed. From each egg case, come April or May, will surge forth many tiny insects. If you find even a single egg case now, you should enjoy the aid and companionship of several mantises in your garden next summer.

In any large patch of blackberries, you are likely to spot the dull brown, knuckle-sized bundles of foam in which the unborn mantids lie. The egg cases may be stuck onto branches or trees or weeds near a thicket, never much higher than eye level. It may take a while to spot the first egg case. But, once you have learned the shape, you will begin to find them more and more easily. You may even discover that you have walked right by one of these inconspicuous treasures in your own backyard.

It is best to store egg cases in a cool, enclosed space. If you put them in the garden now, birds will certainly invade them before summer comes. And, if you bring them indoors, the warmer temperatures invite hatching before the proper time. Remember, in any event, to get the egg case into the garden during the first extended warmth of spring. Otherwise your porch or shed will be crawling with tiny praying mantises.

Later in the summer, you may well run into one of the bright green scavengers that you helped bring into your garden world. Take a moment: look that creature straight in the eye. Catch a glimmer of communion. It may pause, stare back, and seem somehow to signal that you are allies in this vegetative venture.

Wild Onions, Wild Garlic

TAKE a whiff and you know it's an onion. Even in midwinter, wherever strong winds blow the snow away, blue-green patches of chivy wild onions spring up. Come the thaw, these patches proliferate, then swell and flower, come summer. But now their essence dwells underground, in storage bulbs that concentrate flavor

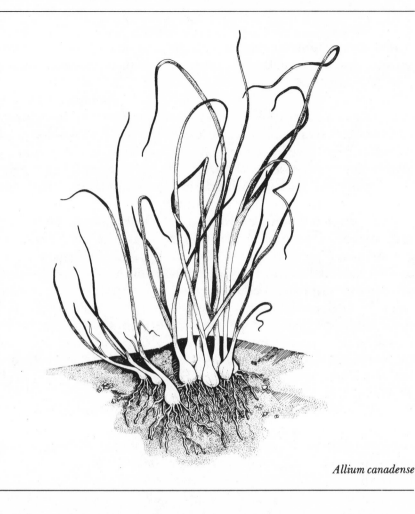

Allium canadense

and nutrients. As long as you can dig two to four inches under, you can dig up onion bulbs through the coming spring.

More than twenty varieties of onions grow wild across the North American continent. All belong to the genus *Allium*—leeks and garlic, onions and shallots, wild and tame alike. Most common and most useful is the native wild onion, *Allium canadense,* with grasslike foliage and small white bulbs. Wild garlic *(Allium vineale)* distinguishes itself with hollow leaves and clinging underground bulblets auxiliary to each plant's central bulbous root. But all the wild onions, as long as they give off that characteristic hot, volatile aroma, can be gathered to add wild punch to lunch.

In winter, one can gather wild onions as one might chives, clipping the tender greenery into salads and soups or freezing the clippings for year-round wild garnish. Try potatoes, boiled and dowsed in butter, rolled in minced wild onion chives. Chopped onion greenery tops a grilled cheese sandwich with pizazz. My favorite winter soup combines sliced sunflower potatoes, wild garlic chives and bulbs, boiled gently in milk and water: simple, seasonal, and nutritious.

As spring eases the growth out of underground bulbs, a flower stalk appears. Often, before the flower forms, I gather a bundle of wild garlic stalks, digging the bulbs out carefully. I snip off the growing end of each stalk. If I didn't, the bulbs could continue to send their energies up into the forming flowers. I've seen wild garlic flower a week after I hung it on the wall to dry. These wild garlic bulbs come in handy throughout the year. They have a taste slightly different from store-bought onions or garlic, for which they can substitute. A bit sharper than commercial onions, a bit milder than garlic, wild garlic bulbs belong in many wild (or tamer) dinner dishes. Many casserole and vegetable dishes take well to the addition of wild onions.

Leave wild onions in the ground and they start to flower. At the growing end of mature stalks, a cluster of tiny pearls develops. In warmer climates, from these pearls emerge onion flowers, blending sweet fragrance with onion pungency. Before they bloom, the pearly flower buds can also be gathered to toss on a salad or casserole or for wild sprouts. Detach at least two tablespoons of wild onion pearls from the flowerheads. Soak them overnight, then keep them in a jar covered with screen or cheesecloth. Keep them warm and dark, and rinse them twice a day. Tiny onion rootlets will emerge, and you can munch on sprouts that combine sharp onion flavor with the high protein value of sprouting seeds.

Nutritionists have discovered another reason for us to include plenty of onions and garlic in the menu. Experiments conducted primarily at universities in India are showing that at least some common members of the *Allium* genus, when combined with other foods, reduce cholesterol levels even when one indulges. Add onion or garlic, cooked or raw, to a menu and you can worry a little less about too much butter or eggs. Most experiments have investigated this quality in cultivated onions and garlic only, but it seems a reasonable hunch that their wild cousins might perform the same service.

Farmers curse the *Allium* species, particularly wild garlic, for earth-clinging roots and runaway bulblets that defy mechanical weeding. Those little cloves keep slipping back into invading fields where compulsive farmers want to grow one plant and one plant only. Wild garlic can ruin a crop of grain. But the goats love the *Allium* species as tasty winter greens. Many a time I've been able to tell what they have been munching just from a whiff of their hot breath. Now I rarely go so far as the goats, chewing wild onion straight from the wild. But I do find the plant conveniently prolific and appropriately mild for cooking almost all year round . . . mild, that is, for an onion.

Winter Terrarium

W H E N snow begins to melt on the mountainside, tiny woodland evergreens show their color again. These plants, which grow naturally in the shady, moist environment of the eastern forest floor, take well to a terrarium. Even in these waning months of winter you can gather a little world of wilderness that will thrive no matter what the weather.

Spotted wintergreen grows abundantly in wooded lots and mountain slopes. Its tough, waxy leaves, rarely more than four or six to a plant, are shaped like those of holly, although they are more slender and irregular in shape. Each jagged leaf is an inch or an inch and a half long and has a white stripe down the center. The plant itself stands no more than four inches above the leaf mold, moss, and lichens with which it shares the forest floor. You may find two or three spent berries rising up on a stem from the central plant. Taut, waxy flowers bloom from spotted wintergreen in summer. Then berries form, white in the warm weather but now browned by winter frost.

Creeping cedar, another plant fit for terrarium life, inhabits predominantly piny surroundings. It weaves an evergreen carpet over the ground where pines drop needles from up above. Each plant bows over and branches out at a height of three or four inches into a filigree fan about three inches across, textured with distinctive cedarlike scales.

I used to encourage the gathering of rattlesnake plantain, a strikingly beautiful woodland evergreen that ranges in similarly mountainous areas. Your terrarium search may turn up many spotted wintergreen plants until that magic moment when the crisp, dark leaves of a rattlesnake plantain appear. A striking sight, its veins bright white, the rattlesnake plantain nestles into rotting trunks and clumps of forest debris. It burrows among fallen leaves as if it were hiding itself from view. And well it may, because this lovely plant is losing the battle against extinction. Marked "threatened" by the federal government, its enemies are commercial wildcrafters who dig the plants and sell them for use in terrariums. In Tennessee alone, according to a Smithsonian report, over half a million plants have been collected for sale. So, excellent as it may be for terrarium use, rattlesnake plantain needs to stay in its wild home. I leave every one I find, admiring it in its native habitat and hoping it will reduplicate its kind.

With all plants, and particularly those considered threatened in their efforts to prolong the species, I try to follow a few simple rituals that keep me from taking more than my share. I never collect the first plant that I find. I prefer to find a group of plants, from which I might take one, leaving plenty to fill in the space I created. Likewise I try to leave ripe seeds or a sprig of root behind, tucked back in under dirt and leaves, so that part of the very plant I plundered may multiply again in its own habitat.

Take a large spoon or trowel on your hunt for terrarium plants, so

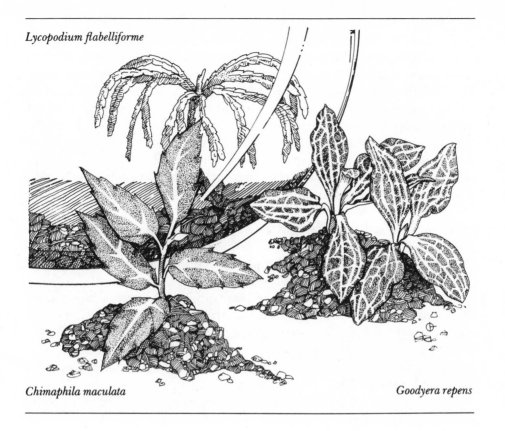

Lycopodium flabelliforme

Chimaphila maculata

Goodyera repens

you can dislodge each plant gently from its forest home. Spotted wintergreen and creeping cedar send long, strong roots outward beneath the leaf mold. The roots never penetrate very deeply into the soil, but they may range four to six inches out from the plant's stem. So take care to uncover an adequate root system and try to grasp a ball of leaf mold and dirt to cushion the roots as you remove them. You can wrap the ball of dirt and roots in large fallen leaves to make it easier to handle.

If you have a big enough basket, carry home some of the good topsoil that enriches these plants naturally. Although I rarely bother, some people treat the woodland soil they gather, to keep creepy crawlers from hatching in their household. An hour's baking at a low oven temperature (200 degrees F., 93 degrees C.) will destroy eggs or organisms. Or you may instead prefer to use predominantly storebought, ready-sterilized soil. It will not be so perfectly suited to your woodland evergreens as the soil in which they were born, but it may be easier to handle and safer over all.

Keep your eyes open for other forest things to set into your terrarium world. Chunks of moss and flaky lichens, colorful pebbles and jagged boughs add depth to that little woodland in a bottle. You don't need to buy a special terrarium to house your forest finds. Of course, an old aquarium will provide space and easy access. But institutional-sized glass jars, often free for the asking at a school or hospital, make fine terrariums too. The wide-mouth jars simply require a slim hand to set in the plants. Those with smaller openings can be penetrated with chopsticks and dexterity.

Begin by preparing the floor of your miniature forest. Collect some stones to line the bottom. These will trap excess water between the crevices and provide ballast if you are using a gallon jar, which you might want to lay on its side. Cover the stones with a layer of charcoal if you have some handy. This also collects extra moisture and keeps the air fresh for the plants.

Next spread a one- or two-inch layer of soil and set the plant roots into it, covering them then with more soil, humus, and leaf mold as you have it. Pack the dirt firmly against the roots for that precious contact between earth and green life. Now you begin to see the tiny forest come alive in a jar. Bumps and dips, twigs and pebbles become the hills and valleys, trees and boulders of your green world. Give the plants a thorough rainshower before you put a cover on. Occasionally, through the coming months, you can open up the terrarium to let in fresh air. But keep it closed and in partial sunlight most of the time. The air inside the jar should always smell fresh and damp, like the forest after a rain.

If you press your ear to the opening just after a thorough watering, you can hear the faint trickle of water percolating through the earth. Like the sea in a seashell, your tabletop terrarium captures a little bit of forest wilderness in a jar.

Gathering Together

T H E T I M E may come in deepest winter when nothing can be gathered. Frost has burned the grass. The wind blows chill. Then snow envelops the landscape. Even winter greens die back. But vestiges of summer growth still stand, silhouetted against bright white. Skeletal stalks whisper hints of what will re-emerge come spring. I try to take advantage of these times of winter dearth because now, more vividly than ever, I gain an overview of the world I gather in.

Although fallen leaves make identification somewhat more difficult, I see the shape and texture of trees so much more clearly in midwinter. The shiny stripes of sweet birch and the mottled brown bark of the sassafras, easing into green, stand out, since now no underbrush surrounds them. I notice a bushy cluster of wild allspice, with speckled bark and tiny yellow globes of flower buds set to awaken in springtime sun. I see a few grapes up there that I missed. Dried and sparse, they might still appeal to the goats, who munch them seeds and all. I give the vine a yank as I walk past.

Poke plants sprawl in clearings where they dominated six months back. Some stalks still stand, but others twist and fall to the ground, their berries dispersed. Sturdy asparagus bushes, the older the stouter, shiver in winter wind. They cling to a few berries, bleached like the foliage. I can just discern the familiar shape of sprouting asparagus where stalk attaches to branches. But the plant passed far beyond that pattern last summer. Now lacy branches protrude. Still I know that just beneath the decay of poke and asparagus in winter lies a root in hibernation. It preserves perennial strength and character, and next spring it will send up a pretty plant. I'll come back, following my memory, to catch the sprouts.

Biennials leave their traces too, promising viable roots and seeds flung near and far to prolong their species. Nubby mullein flower

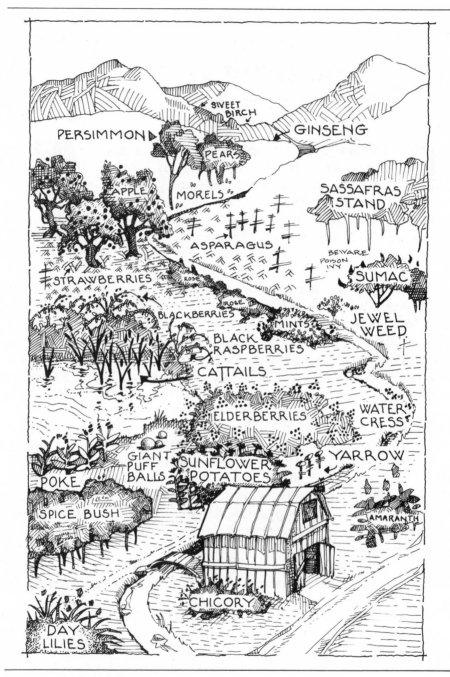

Our gathering places

stalks, brown with frost and age, stand on the hillside. Next spring, flurry florets will sprout alongside them. Naked stalks of rubus berries show up, unencumbered by brush or vines. Now is the time to identify brier patches to cultivate, clearing out spent stalks and preparing for spring mulch.

And though I don't see a sign of fragile annuals—wood sorrel, purslane, and the rest—I know they are down under, in slumber. Seeds cast under summer sun rest quietly in the winter, underground, waiting to hear the call of warmer weather. I know they are there, and I can wait for them, barely able to envision the weed piles and patches that will predominate six months from now.

I like to take advantage of winter starkness to record it all: where the trees take over from the pasture, where poke and asparagus return year after year. I don't claim the skill of a draftsman, but I do claim the joy of a bird on wing as I envision the world of gatherings.

Last winter I made a map of this world. Friends helped. We walked the contours of the land, noting each poke patch and asparagus bush along the way. We noted the apple trees and the persimmons, the sassafras grove, blackberries and black raspberries that the tractor had missed. While we were mapping, we found new stands of cattail and elderberry, earlier hidden in summer overgrowth. I kept the map handy, and we added new details as we saw them. Our final product: an overview of the green and growing world that provides sustenance and health for its human neighbors.

Wild things scatter the world. This whole new world was wild once. Wherever our human grip weakens, wild things flourish once again. The Horticultural Society may have to sow weed seeds in New York City. But weeds carry on, free and strong, just about everywhere else. Today the world seems grim, gray, and bitter cold. But today's map promises the morrow, when we'll go out to gather wild things once again.

Bibliography

ANGIER, BRADFORD. *Field Guide to Edible Wild Plants.* Harrisburg, PA: Stackpole Books, 1974.

BERGLUND, BERNDT, and BOLSBY, CLARE E. *The Edible Wild.* New York: Charles Scribner's Sons, 1971.

BROCKMAN, C. FRANK. *Trees of North America.* New York: Golden Press, 1968.

BROWN, LAUREN. *Weeds in Winter.* Boston: Houghton Mifflin, 1977.

CARLSON, R. F., *et al. North American Apples: Varieties, Rootstocks, Outlook.* East Lansing: Michigan State Press, 1970.

COCANNOUER, JOSEPH A. *Weeds, Guardians of the Soil.* New York: Devin-Adair, 1950.

ELLIOTT, DOUGLAS B. *Roots: An Underground Botany and Forager's Guide.* Old Greenwich, CT: Chatham Press, 1976.

FARMER, MICHAEL and KAY. *The Farmers' Wild Food Recipe Book.* Taylors, S.C.: The Farmers' Way, 1977.

FERNALD, MERRITT LYNDON and KINSEY, ALFRED CHARLES; rev. by Rollins, Reed C. *Edible Wild Plants of Eastern North America.* New York: Harper & Row, 1958 (rev. ed.).

GIBBONS, EUELL. *Stalking the Good Life.* New York: David McKay, 1966.

———. *Stalking the Healthful Herbs.* New York: David McKay, 1966.

———. *Stalking the Wild Asparagus.* New York: David McKay, 1962.

GRIEVE, MAUD. *A Modern Herbal* (2 vols.). New York: Dover Publications, 1971.

HALL, ALAN. *The Wild Food Trailguide.* New York: Holt, Rinehart & Winston, 1976 (rev. ed.).

HARRIS, BEN CHARLES. *Eat the Weeds.* New Canaan, CT: Keats Publishing, 1973.

HATFIELD, AUDREY WYNNE. *How to Enjoy Your Weeds.* London: Frederick Muller, 1969.

HEFFERN, RICHARD. *The Complete Book of Ginseng.* Millbrae, CA: Celestial Arts, 1976.

KIMMENS, ANDREW C., ed. *Tales of the Ginseng.* New York: William Morrow, 1975.

KRAMER, JACK. *The Natural Way to Pest-Free Gardening.* New York: Charles Scribner's Sons, 1972.

KROCHMAL, ARNOLD, WALTERS, RUSSELL S., and DOUGHTY, RICHARD M. *A Guide to Medicinal Plants of Appalachia.* USDA Forest Service (Agriculture Handbook No. 400), 1969.

LEVY, JULIETTE DE BAÏRACLI. *Herbal Handbook for Farm and Stable.* Emmaus, PA: Rodale Press, 1976.

LINSLEY, LESLIE. *Wildcrafts.* Garden City, NY: Doubleday, 1977.

LOVERING, T.G., ed. *Lead in the Environment.* Washington, D.C.: USGPO, 1976.

LUCAS, RICHARD. *Nature's Medicines.* North Hollywood, CA: Wilshire Book Co., 1977 (rev. ed.).

LUST, JOHN. *The Herb Book.* New York: Bantam, 1974.

MCQUARRIE, JACK. *Wildcrafting.* Santa Barbara, CA: Capra Press, 1975.

MARTIN, ALICE A. *All About Apples.* Boston: Houghton Mifflin, 1976.

MEDSGER, OLIVER PERRY. *Edible Wild Plants.* New York: Collier Books, 1966 (rev. ed.).

MELLINGER, MARIE. *"Out of Old Fields . . ."* Rabun Gap, GA: The Hambidge Center, 1975.

MILLER, ORSON K., JR. *Mushrooms of North America.* New York: E. P. Dutton, 1978 (rev. ed.).

NEARING, HELEN and SCOTT. *The Maple Sugar Book.* New York: Schocken Books, 1971 (rev. ed.).

PETERSON, LEE. *A Field Guide to Edible Wild Plants.* Boston: Houghton Mifflin, 1978.

PETRIDES, GEORGE A. *A Field Guide to Trees and Shrubs.* Boston: Houghton Mifflin, 1972 (rev. ed.).

STARÝ, FRANTIŠEK, and JIRÁSEK, VÁCLAV. *Herbs.* London and New York: Hamlyn, 1973.

SHURTLEFF, WILLIAM, and AOYAGI, AKIKO. *The Book of Kudzu.* Brookline, MA: Autumn Press, 1977.

SILVERMAN, MAIDA. *A City Herbal.* New York: Alfred A. Knopf, 1977.

TATUM, BILLY JOE, and WITTY, HELEN, ed. *Billy Joe Tatum's Wild Foods Cookbook and Field Guide.* New York: Workman, 1976.

THOREAU, HENRY DAVID. *Wild Apples.* Boston: Houghton Miffin, 1887.

USDA AGRICULTURAL RESEARCH SERVICE. *Common Weeds of the United States.* New York: Dover Publications, 1971.

VENINGA, LOUISE, and ZARICOR, BENJAMIN R. *Goldenseal/Etc. A Pharmacognosy of Wild Herbs*. Santa Cruz, CA: Ruka Publications, 1976.

WATTS, MAY THEILGARD. *Flower Finder*. N. p.: Nature Study Guild, 1955.

WEINER, MICHAEL A. *Earth Medicine–Earth Foods*. New York: Collier Books, 1972.

WESLAGER, C. A. *Magic Medicines of the Indians*. New York: Signet Books, 1973.

WILKINSON, R. E., and JAQUES, H. E. *How to Know the Weeds*. Dubuque, IA: William C. Brown, 1972 (rev. ed.).

Index

acorns, 130–32
air pollution: lead content in plants, 2, 92, 96
Alderson, John, 94
allspice, wild, 27, 103–05, 128
amaranth, 2, 3, 57, 80, 85–88
American colonists: acorns, 130; allspice, 104; apples, 127; catnip, 61; chickweed, 148; ginger, wild, 133; pennyroyal, 60; poke, 37; purslane, 80; sassafras, 24, 25; self-heal, 101; strawberries, wild, 46; tapping sap, 9; wintercress, 148
Angier, Bradford, 64
antiseptics, 25, 28, 54, 70, 72, 101–03
Aoyagi, Akiko: *The Book of Kudzu*, 89, 91
apples, 71–72, 127–29
Apuleius, 159
"asparagus, Cossack," 64
asparagus, wild, 22–24
astringents, 28, 48, 80, 101, 111, 131, 160
Australian aborigines: cattails used by, 64

bath, floral, 80, 95
berries, rubus, 72–73, 75–76
birch, sweet, *see* sweet birch
birch beer, 12
biscuits: acorn meal, 132; cattail root starch and pollen, 65, 66
black beans, spiced, 134
blackberries, 73
black walnut, 136–37
bouncing bet, 77–79
bread: acorns and acorn meal, 132; amaranth seeds, 86, 87; cattail root starch, 64–65; kudzu starch, 91; persimmon pulp, 156
Brekhman, N., 126
broccoli, wild, 20–21; *see also* wintercress
Brown, Lauren: *Weeds in Winter*, 4

cake: candied violets as decoration, 18; persimmon pulp, 156; sugar plum fruit cake, 156; tart wood sorrel cake, 32
cancer, treatment of, 3, 38, 84, 159–60
candied violets, 17–18
carrot, wild (Queen Anne's lace), 19, 20
catnip, 60–62
cattails, 62, 64–66
chestnuts, 138–39
chickweed, 113–14, 145–49 *passim*, 153
chicory, 3, 21, 105–08, 152, 153
China: ginseng, 121, 122, 124, 125, 126; yarrow, 54, 55
chutney, hobo, 128–29
city weeds/greens, 2, 3
cleansing properties, 77–80; soapwort, 77–79; sumac mouthwash, 111–12; sweet birch for teeth, 12; yucca, 79; *see also* antiseptics
cleavers, 28–30, 80
clovers, 43, 67–69, 98, 108
Cocannouer, J.: *Weeds: Guardians of the Soil,* 21
coffee (substitutes or additions): chicory, 106–08; cleavers, 29; dandelion, 33–35, 108
Cogill, Tom, 75
cole slaw, wild, 81–82, 148
compost, 21, 33, 36
"Cossack asparagus," 64
crabapples, 71–72, 127
creeping cedar, 168, 169
Crowell, Erbin, 59, 146
cultivation and transplanting: amaranth, 88; cattail, 66; chicory, 106, 152, 153, chickweed, 153; compost, 21, 33, 36; indoor gardening, 152–54; insect repellants, plants as, 21, 56, 60–62; mints, 154; onions, wild, 154; periwinkle, 161; poke, 152; praying mantis as natural predator, 162–64; strawberries, wild, 48; sunflower

cultivation and transplanting *(cont'd)*
  potatoes, 146; terrarium, 167–70;
  watercress, 115, 153–54; yarrow, 56, 62; *see
  also* soil
custard and pudding: redbud, 16; rose hip,
  151–52

dandelion, 2, 3, 21, 22–26, 108, 109–10, 152,
  153
daylilies, 51–53
dewberries, 73
drying flowers: Easter egg decoration, 13–15;
  potpourri, 41, 42–43
dyes, onionskin, 15

Easter eggs, decorated and colored, 13–15
elder blow/elderberries, 11, 53, 69–72
Elmore, Sue Anne, 38
evening primrose, 19
evergreens: dyed Easter eggs, 14–15; potpourri, 43; terrarium, 167–70; winter
  wreaths and arrangements, 157–59

Farmer, Michael and Kay *The Farmers' Wild
  Food Recipe Book,* 70
fool's parsley, 19, 20
fried blossoms, 35, 52–53, 70
fritters, elder blow, 70
fruit cake, sugar plum, 156
fruit trees, reviving, 127–29

Gandhi, Mahatma, 80
garden sorrel, 30–31; *see also* sorrels
garlic, wild, 81, 82, 114, 128, 148, 165–66,
  166–67
garnishes, 20, 32, 34, 58, 86, 148, 166; *see also*
  pickles; seeds
Gerard, 101
Gibbons, Euell, 16, 21, 33, 39–40, 82, 95, 119,
  136; *Stalking* books, 3; *Stalking the Wild Asparagus,* 23–24
ginger, wild, 27, 71, 103, 105, 110, 128,
  133–34
ginseng, 98, 102, 121–26
grapes, wild, 118–21
grape vine wreath, 157–59
Grieve, Maud: *Modern Herbal,* 159

Haupt, Margaret, 59
hemlock, poison, 19, 20
hemlock, water, 19, 20
herbal cures, *see* medicinal properties
herbal teas, *see* teas
herbicides, 2, 33, 92
herbs and spices, difference between, 103
hickory, 9, 136, 137–38
hobo chutney, 128–29
Homer, 54

honeysuckle, 43
honeysuckle vine: basket, 15; wreath, 157–59

ice cream: black walnut, 137; redbud blooms,
  16; *see also* syrups
I Ching, 54
identifying plants and trees, 3–4
Indians, 1, 84; acorns, 130, 131, 132;
  amaranth, 85, 87; cattails, 64, 66; chickweed,
  148; ginger, wild, 133; ginseng, 121–22,
  124; may apples, 83–84; pennyroyal, 60;
  poison ivy, 93; poke, 37, 38; puffballs, 118;
  sassafras, 24, 25; sumac, 111; tapping sap, 9;
  wintercress, 148; yarrow, 54; yucca, 79
Indian tobacco, *see* mullein
indoor gardening, 152–54; terrarium, 167–70
insects and pests: natural repellants, 21, 56,
  60–62; pesticides, 2; praying mantis as natural predator, 162–64

jams, jellies, and preserves: elderberry, 71–72;
  grape, wild, 119; may apple marmalade, 83;
  rose hip, 151; spice, 27; violet, 17–18
Japan: daylilies, 53; kudzu, 89
Jaques, H. E.: *How to Know the Weeds,* 4
Jerusalem artichokes, *see* sunflower potatoes
jewelweed, 92–95
Jung, C. G., 54

kudzu, 88–92

Lafitau, Father, 121, 122
lamb's quarters, 2, 3, 53, 56–59, 81–82
Linsley, Leslie: *Wildcrafts,* 15
Lust, John: *The Herb Book,* 4, 115

maple, 8, 11, 12, 13
marmalade, may apple, 83
may apples, 3, 83–85
medicinal properties, 3; catnip, 62; cattail, 66;
  cleavers, 28; clover, 67; dandelion, 33; elder
  blow, 70; ginger, wild, 133, 134; ginseng,
  102, 124–26; jewelweed, 93; kudzu, 89,
  91–92; may apples, 3, 83–84; mullein, 96;
  oak, 131; pennyroyal, 60; periwinkle, 3,
  159–60; poison ivy, 93–94; poke, 3, 37, 38,
  84; puffballs, 118; sassafras, 25, 131; self-
  heal, 101–03; strawberries, wild, 46; sumac,
  80, 111, 131; sweet birch and wintergreen,
  12; violets, 16–17; watercress, 115, 116; yarrow, 54–55, 102
Miller, Orson K., Jr.: *Mushrooms of North
  America,* 4, 117
minerals, *see* vitamins and minerals
"minstrel tea," 60, 160
mints, 43, 53, 60–62, 80, 108–09, 154; *see also*
  catnip; pennyroyal
moonseed, 119–20
morels, 43–45, 116–17

mountain laurel, 157
mouthwash, sumac, 111–12
muffins, acorn, 132
mullein, 3, 96–97, 98
mushrooms, *see* morels; puffballs
mythic and religious properties, 13, 54, 69, 85–86, 121, 122, 124, 125, 126, 127, 159, 160

New York Horticultural Society, 3, 173
nuts/nutting, 136–39; acorns, 130–32

oaks: acorns, 130–32
omelets: garnishes, 34, 58, 86; lamb's quarters, 58–59; morels, 44–45
onions, wild, 154, 164–65, 166–67
onionskin dyes (for eggs), 15
Organic Gardening and Farming Research Center (Emmaus, Pa.), 88
orrisroot, 43

pancakes: elder blow, 70; *see also* syrups
pears, 127–29
pennyroyal, 60, 61, 62, 97–98
perfume (to make), 40, 41–42
periwinkle, 3, 13–14, 15, 60, 159–62
persimmons, 154–56
pests, *see* insects and pests
Peterson, Lee: *Field Guide to Edible Wild Plants*, 3–4
Petrides, George A.: *Field Guide to Trees*, 4
pickles and relishes: daylilies, 51–52; elder bud, 70; evening primrose, 19; hobo chutney, 128–29; poke, 37; purslane piccalilli, 82; spices for, 105 *(see also* allspice, wild; ginger, wild; sassafras); squash or zucchini, 105
pigweed, 56–57, 59; *see also* lamb's quarters
plantain, rattlesnake, 168
poison hemlock, 19, 20
poison ivy, 92, 93–94, 95
poison oak, 93, 94
poisonous or dangerous properties, 1; allspice, wild, 104, 105; carrot, wild, plants resembling, 19–20; elderberry, 70, 72; fool's parsley, 19, 20; grape, wild, plant resembling, 119–20; lead content from polluted air, 2, 92, 96; may apple, 83, 84; moonseed, 119–20; morels, false, 44; mountain laurel, 157; poison hemlock, 19, 20; poison ivy and poison oak, 92, 93, 94, 95; poke, 37, 38–39, 83, 84; puffballs, mushroom resembling, 117–18; safrole, 27; sassafras, 27; snakeberries, 47–48; soapwort, 79; strawberries, wild, plant resembling, 47–48; sumac, 111; watercress in polluted water, 115–16; water hemlock, 19, 20
poison sumac, 111
poke, 3, 36–40, 83, 84, 152

pollution: effects on plants, 2, 92, 96, 113
pomes: reviving old trees, 127–29
potpourri (to make), 41, 42–43, 67
praying mantis, 162–64
puffballs, 116–18
purslane, 2, 3, 57, 80–82

Queen Anne's lace, *see* carrot, wild
quiche, lamb's quarters, 59

rabbit ears, *see* mullein
radish, wild, 19
raspberries, black, 73, 75
raspberries, red, 73, 97
rattlesnake plantain, 168
redbud, 15–16
red clover, *see* clovers
red oaks: acorns, 130–32
religious properties, *see* mythic and religious properties
relishes, *see* pickles and relishes
Rodale, Robert, 88
rose hips, 149–52
roses, 42
Ross, Bertha, 35–36, 75–76
rubus berries, 72–73, 75–76

safrole, 27
Sage, Margaret, 38
salad: amaranth, 81; asparagus, wild, 23; carrot, wild, 20; chickweed, 113–14, 148, 153; chicory, 106; cleavers, 28–29; clover, 67; cole slaw, wild, 81–82, 148; dandelion, 34; daylilies, 51–52; evening primrose, 19; garlic, wild, 81, 114; lamb's quarters, 58, 59, 81–82; onion, wild, 166; purslane, 81–82; radish, wild, 19; redbud, 16; sorrels, 30, 32, 81; sunflower potatoes, 145, 146; violet greens, 16; watercress, 113; winter greens, 114
salad dressings: creamy white, with yarrow, 56, 82; purslane seeds in 82; vinaigrette, 114
sap, collection of, 9, 11–13
sassafras, 24–27, 43, 71, 105, 110, 128, 131
schistosomiasis, 38

seeds (in cooking): amaranth, 81, 86, 87–88; carrot, wild, 20; lamb's quarters, 58, 81–82; purslane, 82; yucca, 79
self-heal, 80, 97, 101–03, 108, 157
"shamrock," *see* wood sorrel
sheep sorrel, 3, 30, 31, 81; *see also* sorrels
Shurtleff, William: *The Book of Kudzu*, 89, 91
skin care: antiseptics, 25, 28, 54, 70, 72, 101–03; astringents, 28, 48, 80, 101, 111, 131, 160; bath, therapeutic, 80, 95; cleansers, 77–80
smokes/smoking, 62, 96–98
snakeberries, 47–48

soapwort (bouncing bet), 77–79
soil, 21; acidic, 21, 30; nitrogen sources, 68–69, 89; sweetened by yarrow, 56, 62; for terrarium, 169–70
sorrels, 3, 21, 30–32, 46, 80, 81
soufflés: poke, 37–38; watercress, 114
soup: additions to, 32, 53, 91; greens and garlic (wintercress), 148–49; morel, cream of, 45; poke, 37; sunflower potatoes, 145; watercress, 114
sparrowgrass, 22
spearmint, 46
spice jelly, 27
spice, wild, *see* allspice, wild
spiced black beans, 134
spices: and herbs, difference between, 103; for pickling, 105
squash, pickled, 105
stew, kudzu and vegetable, 91
strawberries, wild, 46–48, 60, 80, 109, 160
sugar maple, *see* maple
sumac, 11, 80, 111–13, 131, 157
sunflower potatoes, 143–46
sweet birch, 9, 11, 12, 13, 27
Syracuse University, 66
syrups: grape, wild, 119; maple, 9, 11, 12, 13; violet, 16, 18

tapping trees, 9, 11–13
Tatum, Billy Joe: *Wild Foods Cookbook and Field Guide,* 4
teas, 108–10; allspice, wild, 104; amaranth, 80; catnip, 62; cattail, 66; cleavers, 28, 29, 80; clover, 67–68; 108; dandelion, 109–10; elder blow/elderberry, 70, 72; ginger, wild, 110, 134; ginseng, 102, 123, 124; jewelweed, 95; kudzu, 92; "minstrel tea," 60, 160; mints, 80, 108–09; oak (acorn), 131; pennyroyal, 60, 160; periwinkle, 60, 160; rose hip, 150, 151; sassafras, 25–27, 110, 131; self-heal, 80, 102, 108; sorrels, 32, 46, 80; spearmint 46;

strawberry, wild, 46, 48, 80, 109, 160; sumac, 80, 112–13, 131; sweet birch, 12; violet, 18, 109; yarrow, 54–55, 60, 80, 102, 108
tempura, 52–53
terrarium (to make), 167–70
Thoreau, Henry David, 127–28
tomatoes, green, with wood sorrel, 32
tonics, 25–27, 55, 102, 124–26
transplanting, *see* cultivation and transplanting
trefoil, *see* wood sorrel

violets, 13–18 *passim,* 109
vitamins and minerals, 2, 21, 110; amaranth, 2, 86; chicory, 21, 106; dandelion, 2, 21, 33; lamb's quarters, 2, 57–58; poke, 39; purslane, 2, 82; rose hips, 150; sap, 11; strawberries, wild, 46; sunflower potatoes, 145; violets, 16; watercress, 113, 115

waffles: cattail root starch in, 65; persimmon, 156; *see also* jams, jellies, and preserves; syrups
walnut, 9
walnut, black, 136–37
watercress, 53, 113–16, 152, 153–54
water hemlock, 19, 20
Watts, May Theilgard: *Flower Finder,* 4
white oaks: acorns, 130–32
Wilkinson, R. E.: *How to Know the Weeds,* 4
wine: dandelion, 35–36; grape, wild, 120–21; rubus berry, 75–76
wintercress, 20–21, 145, 147–49
wintergreen, 12, 160, 167–68, 169
wood sorrel, 3, 31–32; *see also* sorrels
wreath, winter, 157–59

yarrow, 53–56, 60, 62, 80, 97, 102, 108, 157
yucca, 79

Zaricor, Ben, 27
zucchini, pickled, 105